In Search of a Beautiful Sky

A Spiritual Journey of Enlightenment Through Photography

Bill Caldwell

ABeautifulSky Photography

In Search of a Beautiful Sky
A Spiritual Journey of Enlightenment Through Photography

Published 2019, by ABeautifulSky Photography

www.ABeautifulSky.com
Cottonwood, Arizona 86326 USA

Cover design by Bill Caldwell
Photographic art by Bill Caldwell/ABeautifulSky Photography

ISBN (Paperback): 978-0-9600585-0-1
ISBN (E-Book): 978-0-9600585-1-8
Library of Congress Control Number: 2019908892

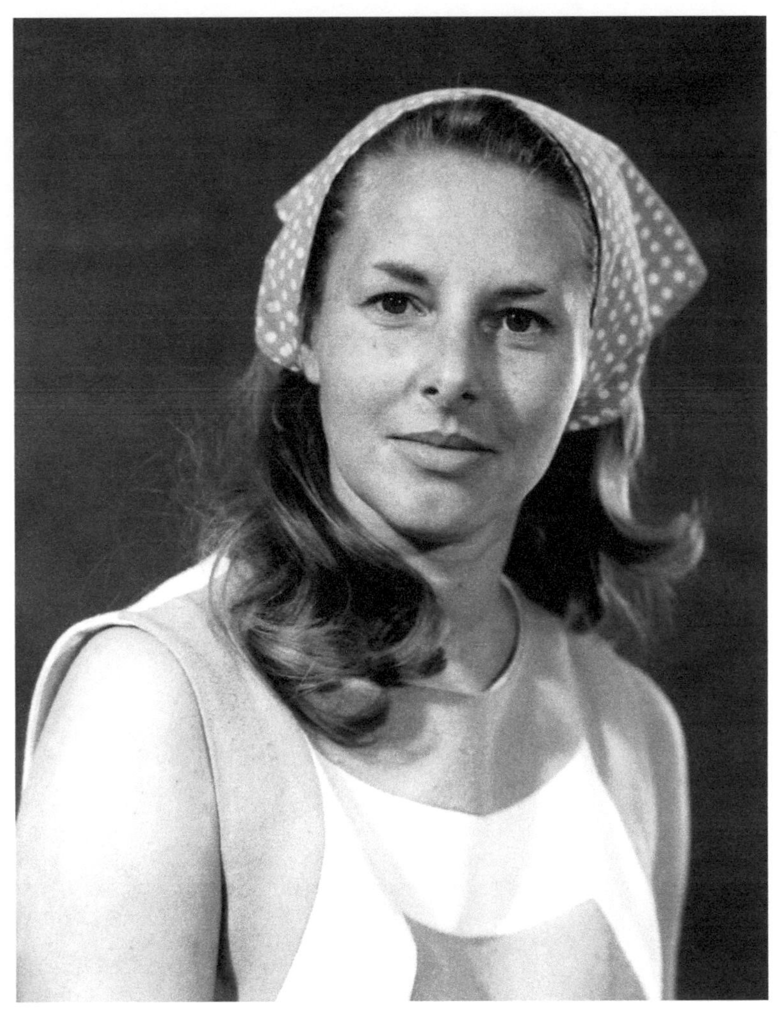

Chris Caldwell

Dedicated to my stepmom, Chris.
She planted the seeds of metaphysics and true spirituality when I was a boy.
Her kind loving nature made all the difference.

Listen to Your Heart

Sit in nature and be present.

Listen to the birds sing,
for they are free and live in the light.

Listen to the wind sing,
for it carries the truth far and wide.

Listen to the trees sing,
for they have much to teach us.

Listen to the rocks sing,
for the Earth is ancient and wise.

Listen to the water sing,
it will show you the way home.

Sit in nature and listen to your heart sing,
it is your song,
it is your story,
it is your path.
Sit in nature and hear your heart!

PREFACE

The purpose of this book is to share my spiritual journey along with my photographic art of the beautiful natural places I've visited and my artistic vision of those places. This is not a complete autobiography (that would be too long and boring) but rather a collection of memorable events and crossroads that helped shape my spiritual journey and my beliefs. This is also the story of what I've learned and come to believe.

So why would anyone want to read a book by Bill Caldwell? I'm not a celebrity and I'm not a New York Times best-selling author. I'm 63 years old and I spent 20 years in the US Air Force as a Combat Search and Rescue (CSAR) navigator. Now I'm pursuing my love of landscape and artistic photography along with my enduring interest in spirituality. I've never written a book before, so why did I write this book? Soon after I got my BA Degree in photography (about 41 years ago) I started dreaming about publishing a book with my pictures of nature. So I've had this vision of publishing a book like this for many years, but I never really knew what I would write about—that is, until recently. My wife suggested that I write about my spiritual journey and I realized that over the years my photography has changed quite a bit, along with my spiritual beliefs and attitudes. I truly believe that one of the reasons we are all here in the physical world is for the purpose of spiritual growth and expansion, and I thought that other people who are also on a spiritual path would be interested in my story.

For me, hiking and connecting with nature is an important part of my spiritual path, as well as my general well-being, and I suspect this is also true for many others. One of the definitions of the word sacred is "worthy of or regarded with reverence, awe, or respect." In this sense, I consider these beautiful natural areas as sacred ground. I feel a strong spiritual connection to the land so my photographic art comes from a place of profound reverence and appreciation for this beautiful planet Earth. As a photographic artist, my primary intention is always to create beautifully uplifting pictures, and to communicate my feeling of awe and wonder when I explore and photograph the incredible spacious beauty of the natural world.

I like something that Sylvia Brown says at the beginning of her books: "Take what you like and leave the rest." In other words, if what I'm writing resonates with you, great, if not, feel free to disregard the parts that don't. Or, as Bruce Lee said, "Adapt what is useful, reject what is useless, and add what is specifically your own." I'm not trying to sell you on my particular beliefs, I just want to share some of my experiences and lessons learned along my spiritual path, and possibly inspire others to keep an open mind while finding their own spiritual path, their own "path with a heart."

If there's anything I've learned during my life, it's that there is much more going on in the world and the universe than meets the eye. Much more going on than our five senses or scientific instruments will show us, much more than any religion will tell us, much more than most people are aware of or can imagine. The universe is a fantastic and mysterious place. This is my story.

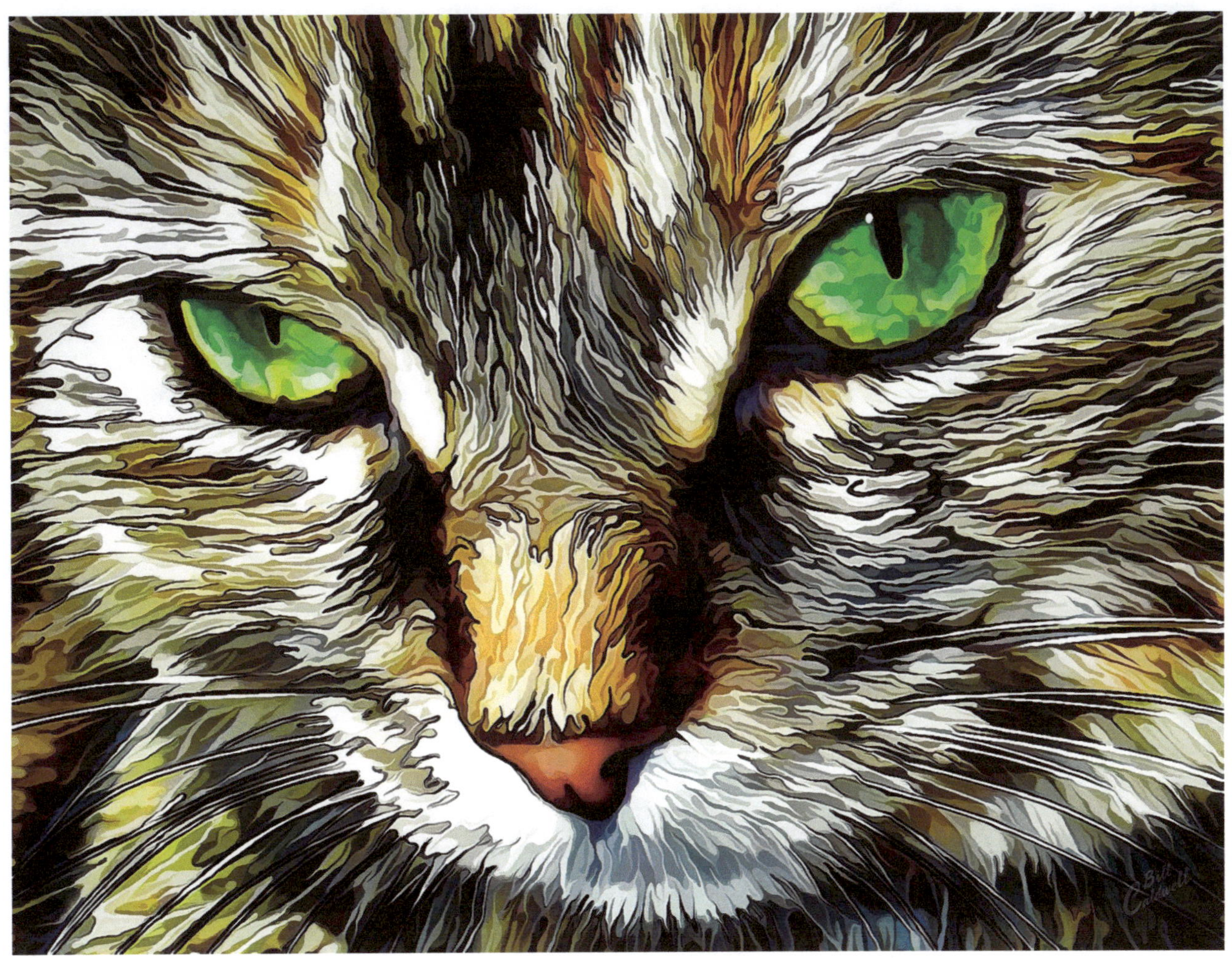

Destiny Caldwell
My zen master, teacher, and all-around helper.

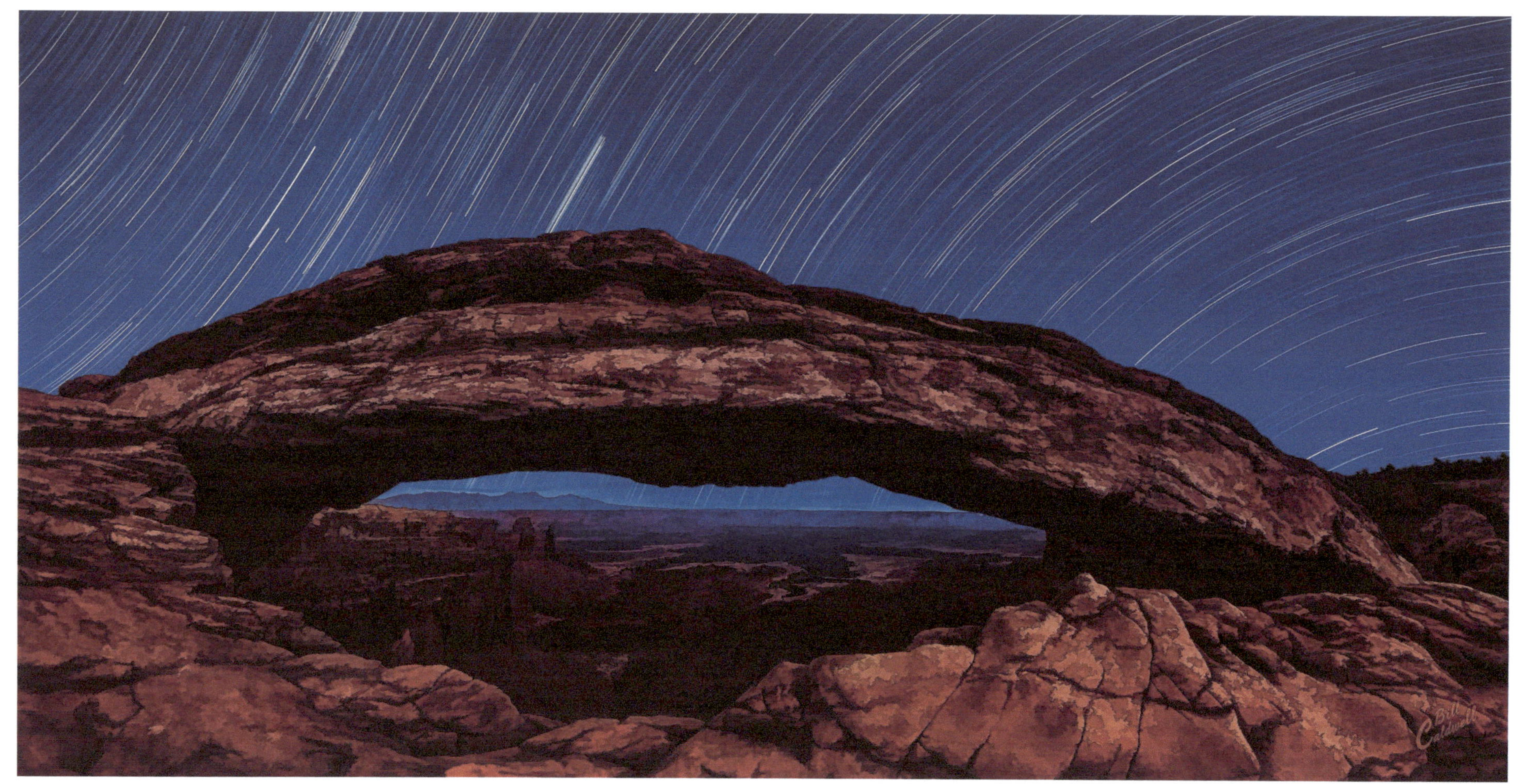

Dimensional Gateway

"I'll tell you one thing about the universe, though. The universe is a pretty big place. It's bigger than anything anyone has ever dreamed of before. So if it's just us...seems like an awful waste of space. Right?"
— Ellie Arroway "Contact"

Part 1
My Story

You could say I was born asking questions. Like most children, I was very curious about pretty much everything. I loved learning new things in school, and I especially loved going exploring outside after school. I would ride my bike and hike all over the place, mostly in the nearby hills, canyons, coastline, and any undeveloped areas outside of my neighborhood. I grew up in Southern California during the 60s and looking back now, I realize how lucky I was to have lived near natural, undeveloped areas and coastal areas, as well as having the freedom to explore. I also wanted to know how things work, why people do what they do, why we are here, where we came from, where we are going, etc, etc. Later on, my curiosity included physics, astronomy, cosmology, religion, spirituality, metaphysics, engineering, photography, psychology, and more.

I started reading books at an early age—mostly adventure stories like the Hardy Boys at first. Then a friend introduced me to science fiction, and wow, that really captured my imagination and opened my mind to new possibilities! I was fascinated by the idea that other beings, other cultures, and other worlds might exist in the universe. The idea that humans on planet Earth are the only intelligent life amongst the billions of stars, planets, and galaxies seemed ridiculous. I devoured many sci-fi novels by authors like Isaac Asimov, Arthur C. Clarke, Robert Heinlein, and many others. Through these stories (and my imagination) I was able to travel to distant planets, stars, and galaxies throughout the universe. All these sci-fi stories also opened my mind to different ideas and beliefs about culture, society, government, religion, spirituality, and philosophy. They also sparked my interest in the sciences like astronomy, cosmology, and physics.

The interesting thing is that when I was in the second grade I was failing reading and arithmetic. My parents had gone through a divorce the previous year and I was living with my biological mother along with my brother and two sisters in the San Diego area. My brother and I (about ten and seven years old at the time) were pretty much running wild in the streets with very little supervision. I remember one time when we snuck into the back of a restaurant and stole a whole roasted chicken that was sitting on the counter cooling down. We really had no sense of responsibility and little sense of right and wrong. We we're just kids and we were on the verge of becoming juvenile delinquents.

Shortly after that, my father remarried and gained custody of us. We moved up to the Los Angeles area to live with him and my new stepmom, Chris. As it turns out, Chris was a godsend—I consider her to be my personal savior. Looking back, this was a very important turning point in my life. Her bubbly personality and kind loving nature made all the difference in the world. For the first few months I clung to her like a lost puppy starved for affection. Talk about quality time, Chris spent many hours with me after dinner helping me with my reading and arithmetic. This is when my love of reading began and later on it became so important in my spiritual journey. Of course, reading and mathematics also became very important later on when I joined the U.S. Air Force and became a search and rescue navigator.

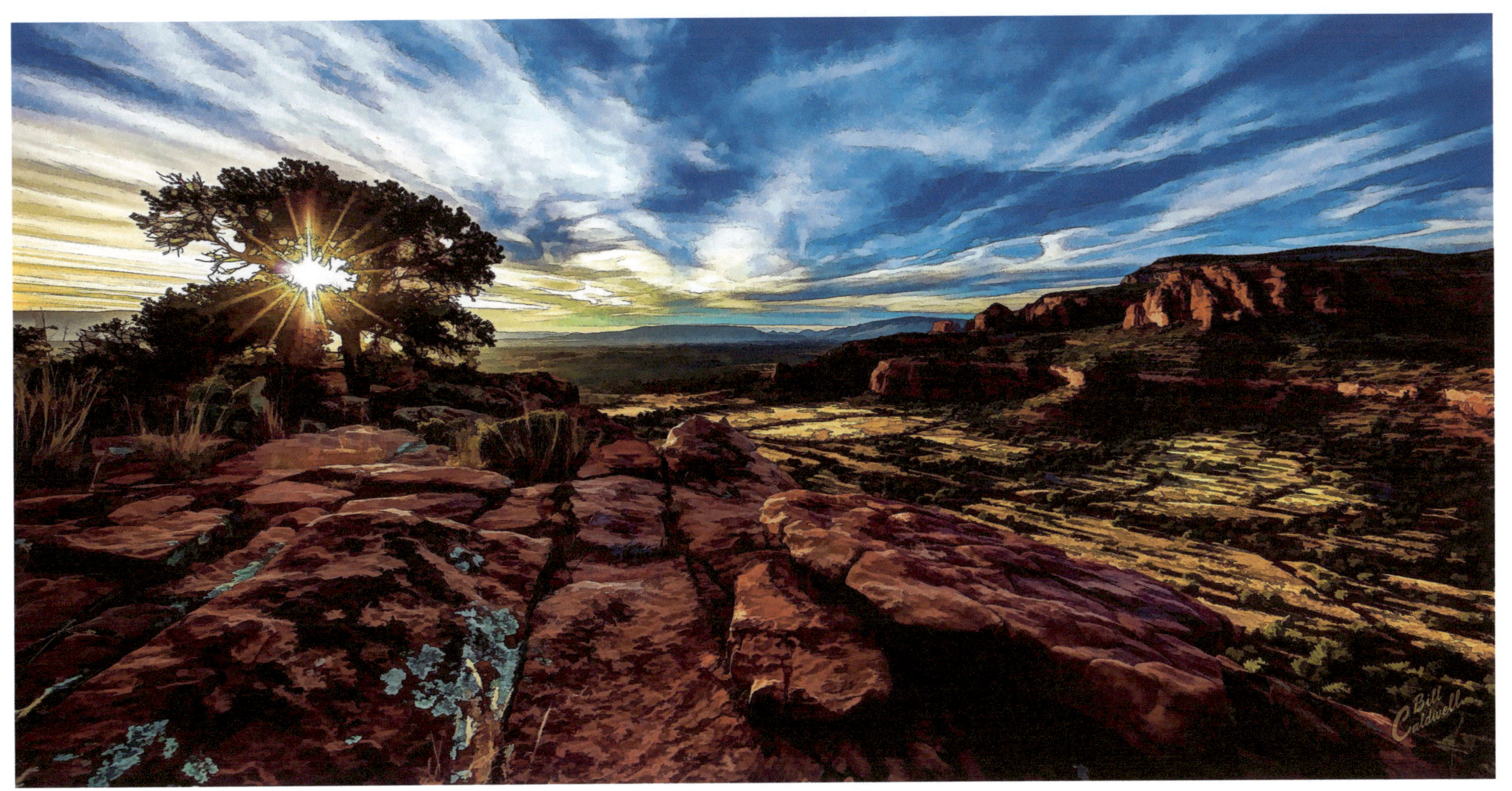

Pathway to the Light

Find your path to the light—there is no greater purpose than this.

Lucky for us kids, my dad loved going to the beach and swimming in the ocean—snorkeling, scuba diving, and riding the waves on inflatable mats at first, and then graduating to surfboards later on. This was great fun for us kids and introduced us to another beautiful side of nature at an early age. My dad was also interested in photography and built his own underwater housings so he could take pictures and movies of his scuba diving adventures. I used to love watching his slideshows and movies of the underwater world. Around this same time I received a Polaroid Instamatic camera for my birthday which I really loved, so this was my first introduction to photography. I also loved watching the TV series "The Undersea World of Jacques Cousteau." This is when I really began to appreciate the beauty of the natural world and truly understand the importance of preserving and protecting our environment. For me, snorkeling and scuba diving is like visiting an incredible alien planet. The underwater world is so diverse and beautiful and so completely different from the surface environment. My little world began expanding along with my sense of awe and wonder.

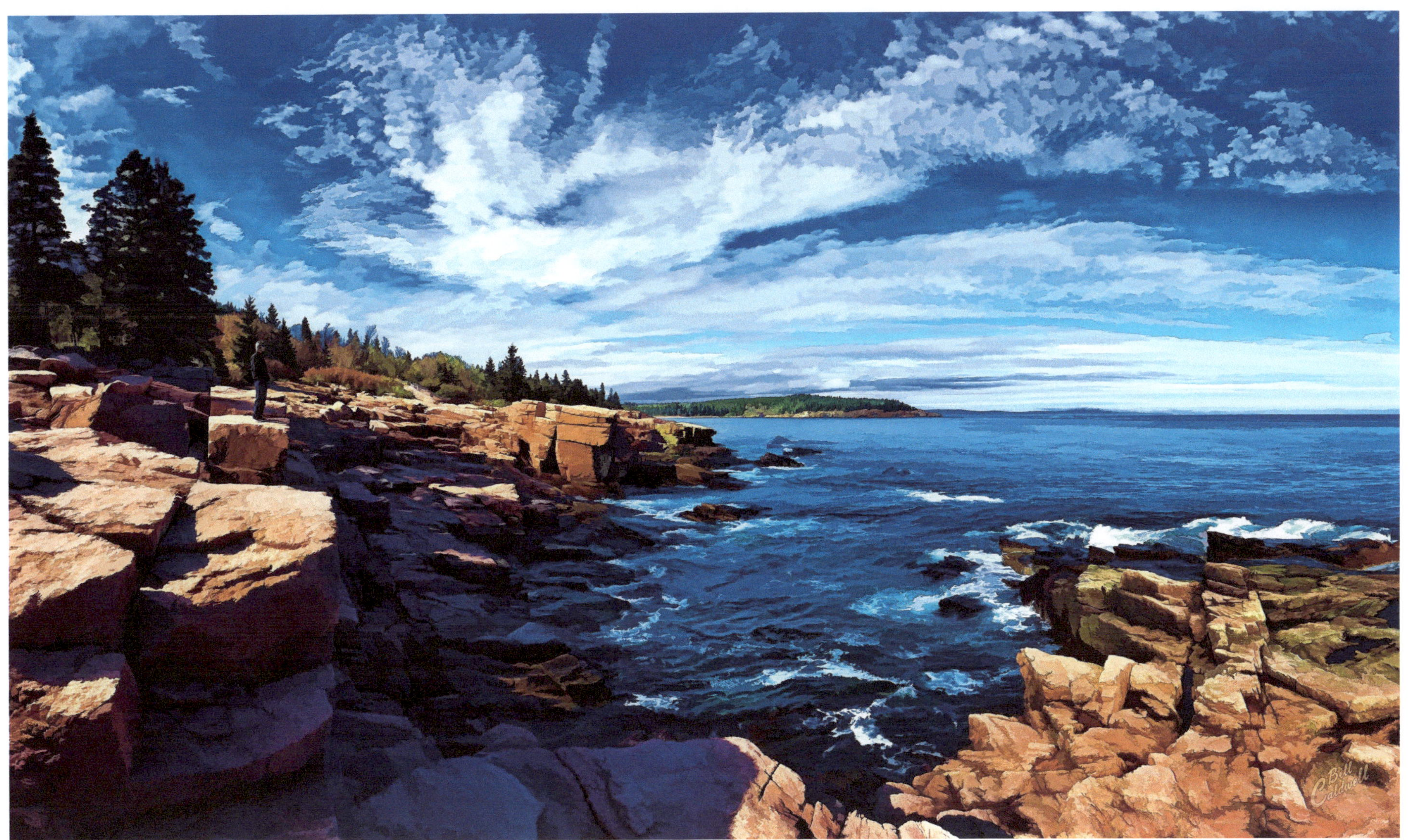

Ocean Wonder

"The Sea, once it casts its spell, holds one in its net of wonder forever."
— Jacques Cousteau

Although I didn't understand it at the time, I got my first lesson in the effects of prejudice, labels, and ego identification during the fourth grade. My best friend was of Japanese descent but, of course, we were just kids and we didn't care about such differences. That is, until one night there was a movie on TV about World War II in the Pacific theater and the war against the Japanese. We both saw the movie and the next day we talked about the movie and ended up in an argument. From then on, he was "Japanese," I was "American," and our friendship ended. For the rest of the day, and a long time after that, I felt baffled and confused along with the sting and sadness of losing a friend. I kept replaying the argument in my mind over and over again but I couldn't figure out what had happened. I wasn't blaming him or his family personally for Pearl Harbor, but I think it must have sounded that way to him. I realize now that our egoic minds were developing and we each identified with being "Japanese" or "American," and in the context of that World War II movie, we were "enemies." Another brick in the shell of our egos. His family moved away soon after, and I never saw him again.

Many years later I would read Eckhart Tolle's book "A New Earth" and I finally began to understand the difference between ego, personality, and our authentic self. It occurred to me that the ego is a little bit like the leaves on a tree. As we are growing up, as children and especially during the teenage years, this protective shell of the ego grows around us, surrounding us like the leaves of a tree. When you strip away all those leaves, all those ego identifications, what you find at the core of your being is your authentic self.

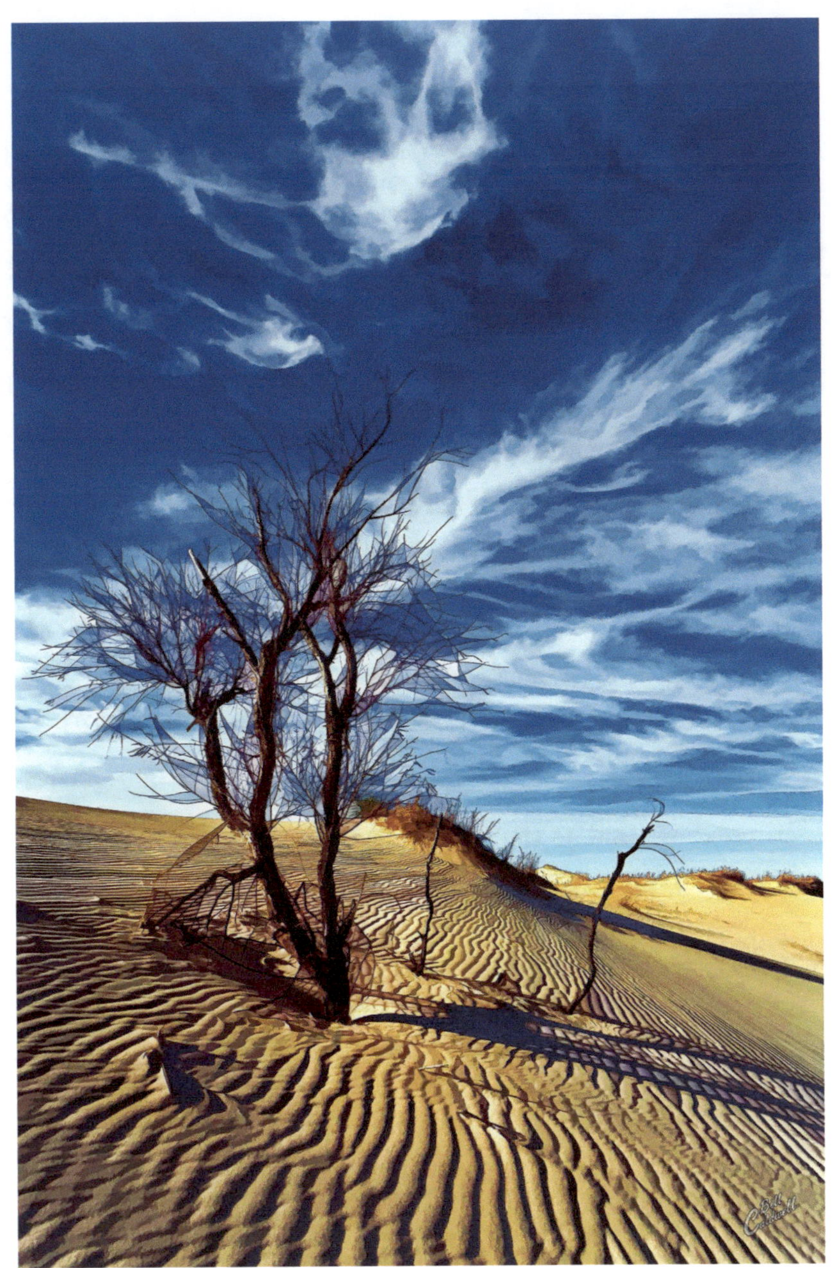

Circle of One

"The most common ego identifications have to do with possessions, the work you do, social status and recognition, knowledge and education, physical appearance, special abilities, relationships, personal and family history, belief systems, and often nationalistic, racial, religious, and other collective identifications. None of these is you."
— Eckhart Tolle

While I was going to elementary school, we lived close enough so I could ride my bike to school every day. But once I graduated elementary school, I had to start taking the bus because the junior high was much farther away. One day something very strange and frightening happened to me while I was walking to the bus stop. I had to walk about three blocks and cross a busy main street to get to the bus stop. There were no other children that lived close to me that were going to the same junior high, so I would walk alone through the quiet neighborhood. One day I was walking along completely lost in thought, looking down at my feet as I went along, and all of a sudden something caused me to stop suddenly. I had stopped so quickly that it felt like I had just run into a wall. I started to look up, wondering what had caused me to stop, when a white car went flashing past me in a blur. It passed within inches of me and all I could see was a momentary glimpse of a portion of the passenger window, the white door, and the chrome door handle. The hair on the back of my neck stood on end and a chill ran through my body. If I had kept walking I would've been run down and seriously injured, if not killed outright. I then realized that I had reached the main road and had started crossing it without looking for traffic because I was so lost in thought and looking down at my feet. What just happened? I was very shaken by this experience and for a long time I wondered what had stopped me. Looking back on it now, I truly believe that one of my spirit guides or some sort of guardian angel stopped me—truly a case of divine intervention. This was not the first time something inexplicable like this happened to me, and it would not be the last. This was also one of the first times that I realized there was much more going on in the world then meets the eye, more than what you can perceive with your five physical senses.

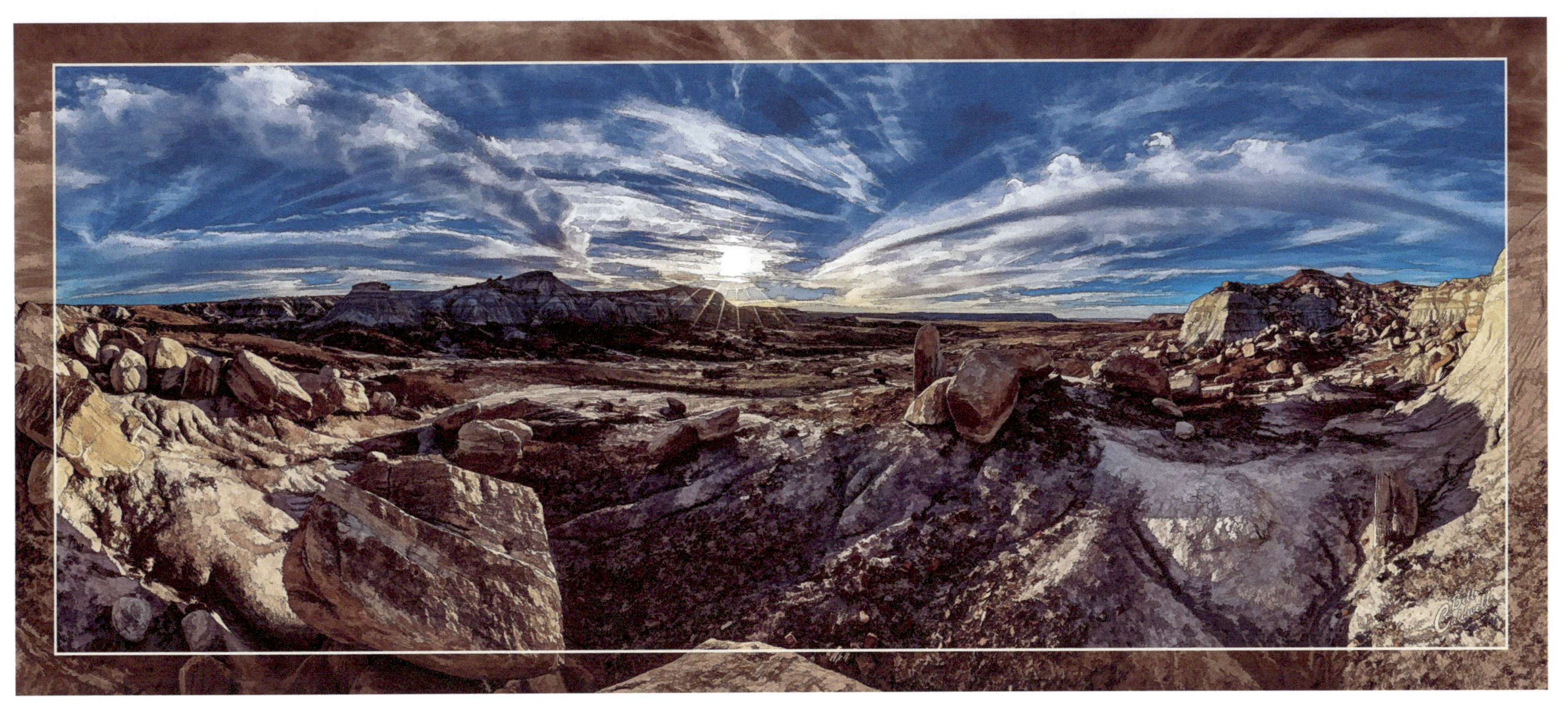

Divine Purpose

Know that you are loved. Know that every life is important to the divine purpose of the Universe!

Our family would often spend weekends at the beach, and sometimes during the summer, my dad would drop my brother and I off at the beach on his way to work. When I was about 12 years old I graduated from belly boarding to stand up surfing. Up until then I had been riding the waves lying down on a small belly board about 3 feet long. At that time surfing was going through a transition from long boards to short boards. In the previous years, surfboards were quite large, in the 10 to 12 foot range and quite heavy. By the time I started surfing, the surfboards were becoming smaller—somewhere in the 7 to 8 foot range and much lighter weight. My Dexter belly board was made in the same way but years later belly boards would be replaced by the ubiquitous "boogie board." I decided that I was going to teach myself how to stand up surf on my little 3 foot belly board. Stand up surfing on such a small board was unheard of back then (even for a child) but I had this vision and I was convinced that if I could build up enough speed on a wave that I could stand up on my little belly board without sinking. As it turns out, I was right. After much trial and error, and many failed attempts, I was able to ride a wave standing up on my belly board—WooHoo! I was so excited and exhilarated by this experience! Surfing became my passion for many years, and anytime I could get to the beach, after school or after work, you would find me out in the water… surfing.

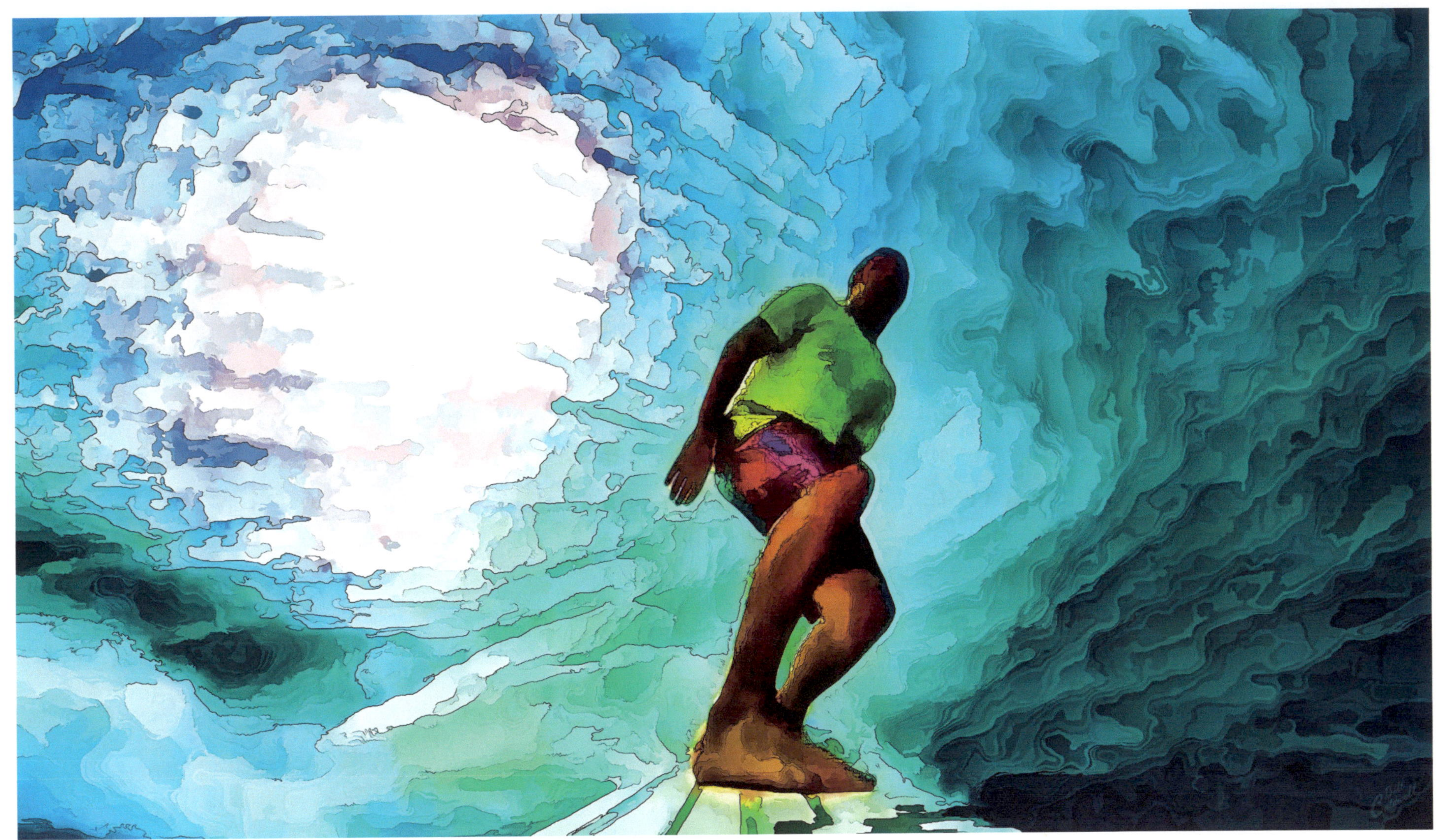

Go With The Flow

Find your joy, let go of resistance, and go with the flow of the energy of your life.

When I was in junior high, besides reading sci-fi novels and books about the sciences, I started reading books about philosophy, metaphysics, and spirituality. The first of these books was "The Prophet" by Khalil Gibran which my stepmom Chris had. Some of the passages from this book resonated with me and inspired me to read other books like "Walden" by Henry David Thoreau and "Autobiography of a Yogi" by Paramahansa Yogananda. I was becoming more introspective, and this is when I really started wondering about why we are here, what my purpose is, what happens when we die, what religion is, what spirituality is, and if there is more to life than just eating, sleeping, and working to make a living.

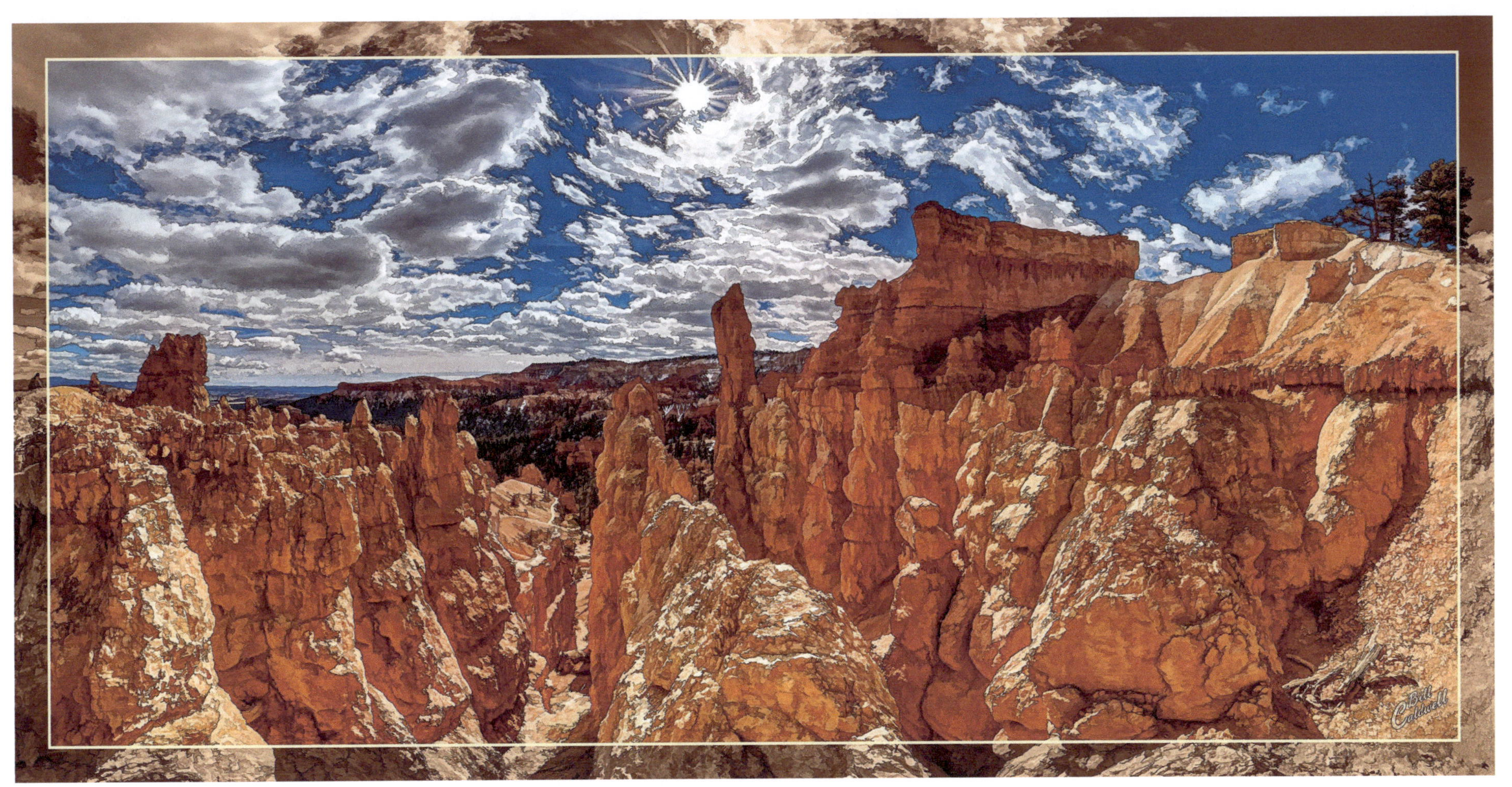

Look Within

"Introspection is the examination of one's own conscious thoughts and feelings. In psychology, the process of introspection relies exclusively on observation of one's mental state, while in a spiritual context it may refer to the examination of one's soul. Introspection is closely related to human self-reflection and is contrasted with external observation." (Wikipedia)

I also took a photography class when I was in junior high, one of the few elective classes available. Little did I know what a huge affect this would have on my life. Actually, I took this class twice and also took an extra bonus class that was being offered by a local professional photographer. I loved taking pictures, and at first I was taking pictures of pretty much anything and everything. After a while though, I started focusing more and more on nature, both close-ups and landscapes. My dad knew the basics of photography, and when he saw how intrigued I was, he helped me build a small dark room in our garage so that I could process my own black and white film and prints. Once I learned the basics of processing and printing, I started experimenting with artistic photographic effects like solarization and photo posterization. I also experimented with infrared photography, and I was fascinated by the idea that you could create pictures using a wavelength of light that was not visible to the human eye. This was a huge turning point in my life. Photography really captivated me—captivated my curiosity, my imagination, and my creativity. From then on, photography became an integral part of my life. Although I never made a living from photography, it was a very important part of my creativity and joy, and was just as important as the work I did to make a living.

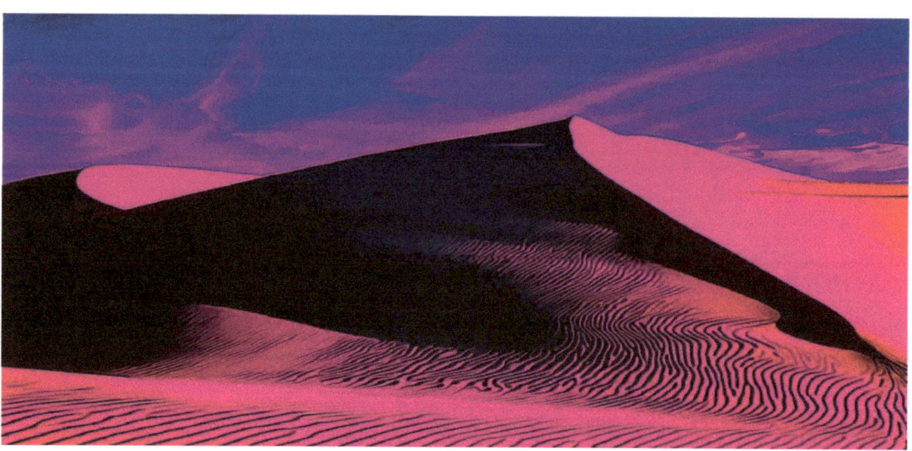

Infrared Sand Dune

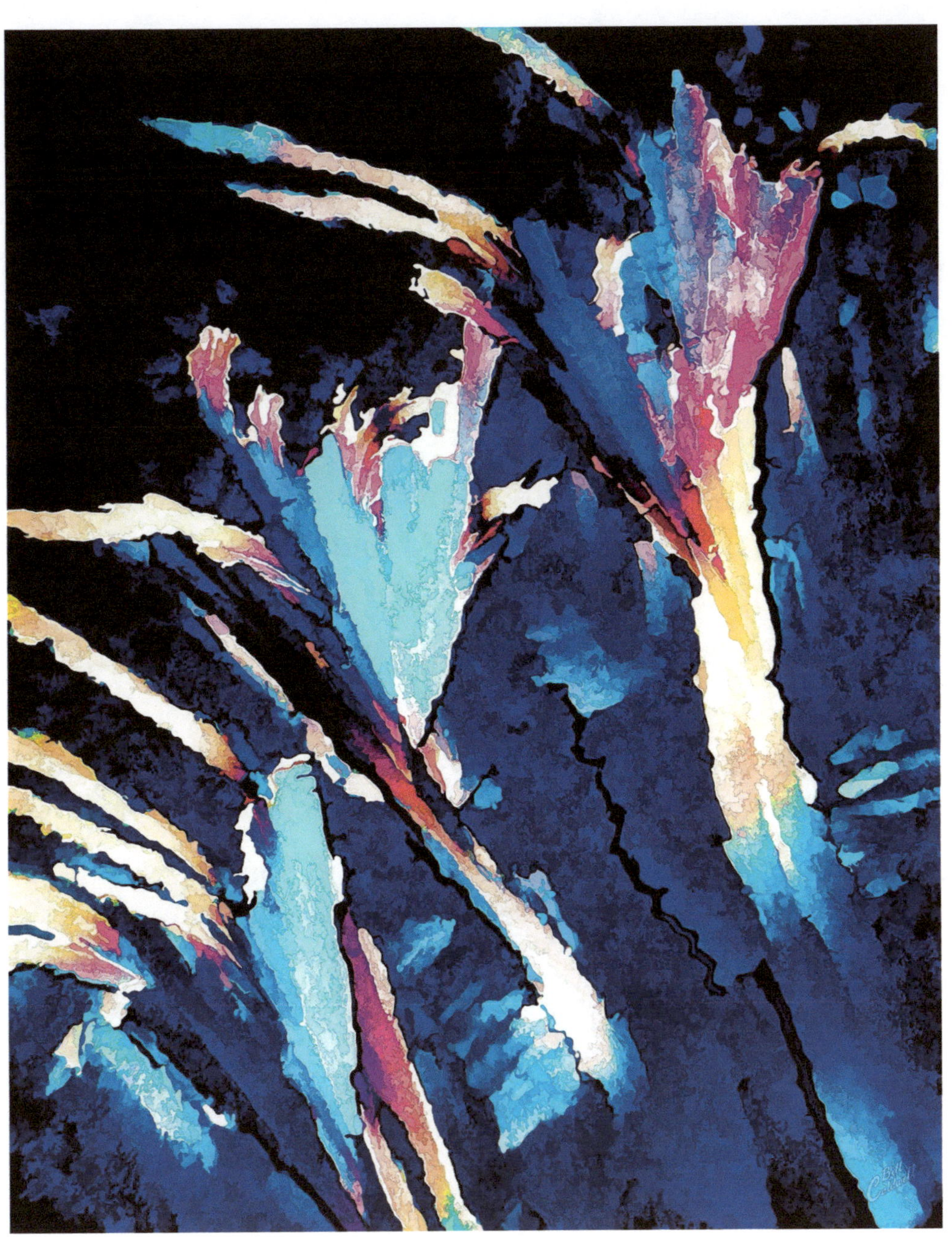

Crystal C Abstract

The more engaged I became in photography, the more it changed how I looked at the world. I became more conscious of the light; the angle of the light, the textures it revealed, the color quality of the light, and the position of the sun during different times of the day and the changing seasons. I was also fascinated with macro and micro photography—taking pictures of very small subjects and magnifying them—like crystalized vitamin C through a microscope. When my family took a road trip and we stopped at a scenic overlook, they teased me because I had to stop and take a close-up picture of a tiny flower by the pathway before going on to see the majestic overlook.

"The inspiration you seek is already within you. Be silent and listen."
— Rumi

In high school I was still very interested in metaphysical and spiritual subjects as well as the physical sciences like astronomy, physics, and chemistry. Astronomy especially fascinated me—the structure of the solar system, the galaxy, and the whole universe, as well as black holes, neutron stars, supernovas, and nebulas. I loved looking at astronomical pictures of the beautiful planets, nebulae, and galaxies. I was also fascinated by the mechanics and physics of how stars are formed and how they produced so much light and energy, as well as how black holes are formed and how they behave. One of my favorite TV programs was a thirteen-part television series on PBS, "Cosmos: A Personal Voyage," presented and narrated by Carl Sagan. For me, learning about astronomy and physics was a form of spirituality because it gave me a bigger perspective and an expanded sense of the universe. There are literally billions of galaxies in our physical universe and within each of those galaxies there are, on average, about a hundred billion stars. The size and scale of the universe is absolutely staggering. Our solar system alone is over 7 billion miles across. Seeing the incredible immensity of our solar system and our Milky Way galaxy, let alone the overall universe, gave me such a sense of awe and wonder, and of humility, seeing how small our little world is in comparison.

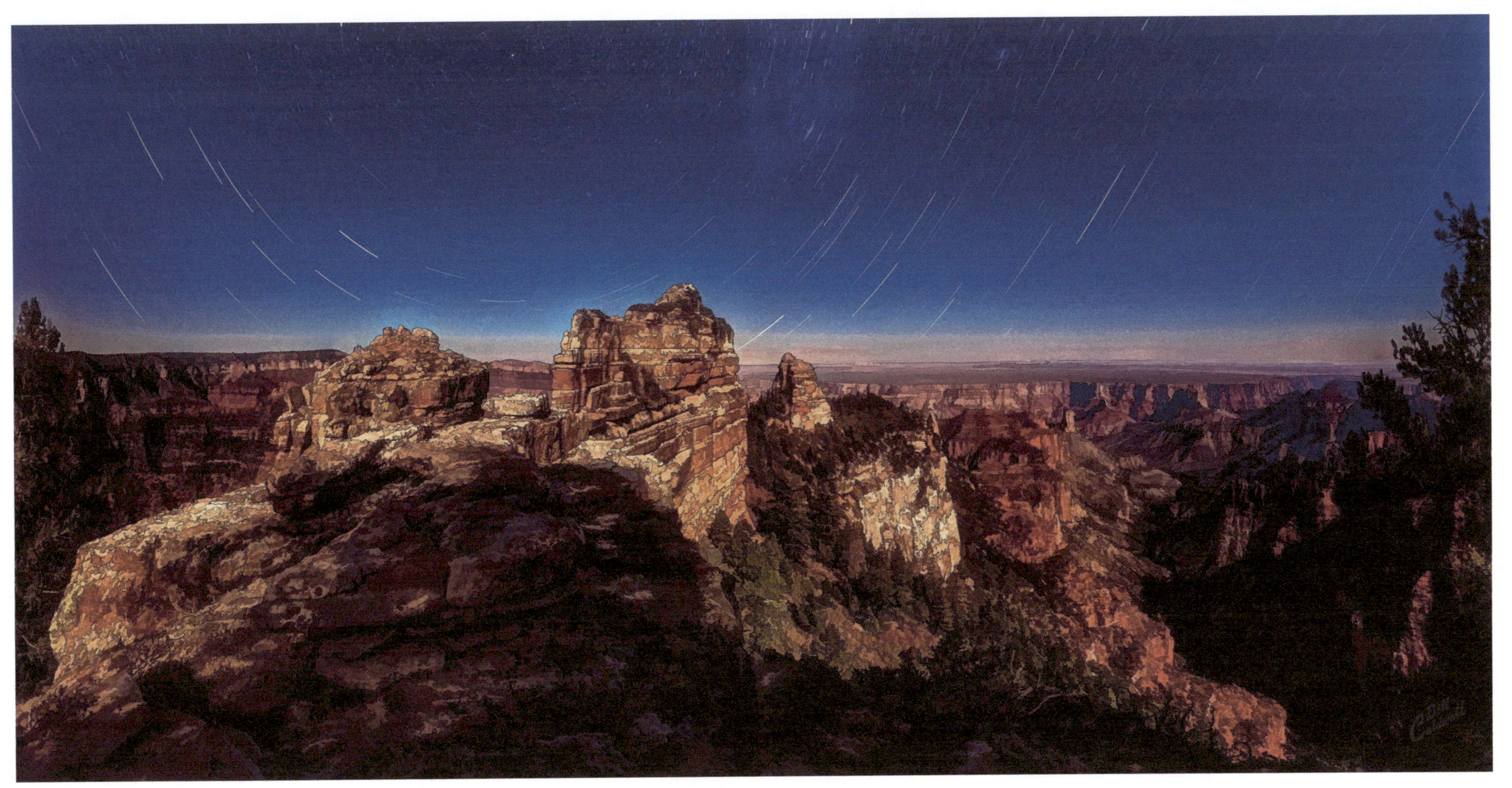

Sacred Passage

"Science is not only compatible with spirituality, it is a profound source of spirituality.
When we recognize our place in an immensity of light-years and in the passage of ages,
when we grasp the intricacy, beauty, and subtlety of life, then that soaring feeling,
that sense of elation and humility combined, is surely spiritual." — Carl Sagan

One of my favorite classes in high school was a class called General Semantics and Epistemics. My teacher was named Verlin Heuton (by far my favorite high school teacher) and he taught from the book "The Art of Awareness: A Textbook on Epistemics and General Semantics" by J. Samuel Bois. This was a fascinating class where we explored, among other things, the mental processes of cognition and how we perceive the external world, our thoughts and perceptions of past, present, and future, as well as how our language affects our perceptions and thought processes. We also looked at transcendental meditation, social psychology, psychological attitudes, and various philosophies, with lots of interesting discussions and practical exercises. This class was very, very different from any of my other high school classes and opened my mind to a whole new world—a whole new way of *looking* at the world. Taking this class taught me the value of keeping an open mind and a willingness to look at other possibilities that seem to be outside the realm of what I thought possible. This class was a very important part of my spiritual journey, expanding my awareness and paving the way for my future growth and expansion.

Because of this class, I started reading the series of books by Carlos Castaneda about his experiences as an apprentice with a Yaqui indian and shaman, don Juan Matus. In his first book, Carlos quotes don Juan about "a path with a heart" and this quotation resonated with me so deeply that I've kept it with me ever since. Don Juan explained that before any important decision, one should ask: "Is this a path with a heart?" He also explained that "a path with a heart" is not a lifelong commitment, that any path may be temporary, and when you reach the end of that path, then it's time to find the next "path with a heart." This was in 1973 and every major decision I've made since that time was influenced by this quote.

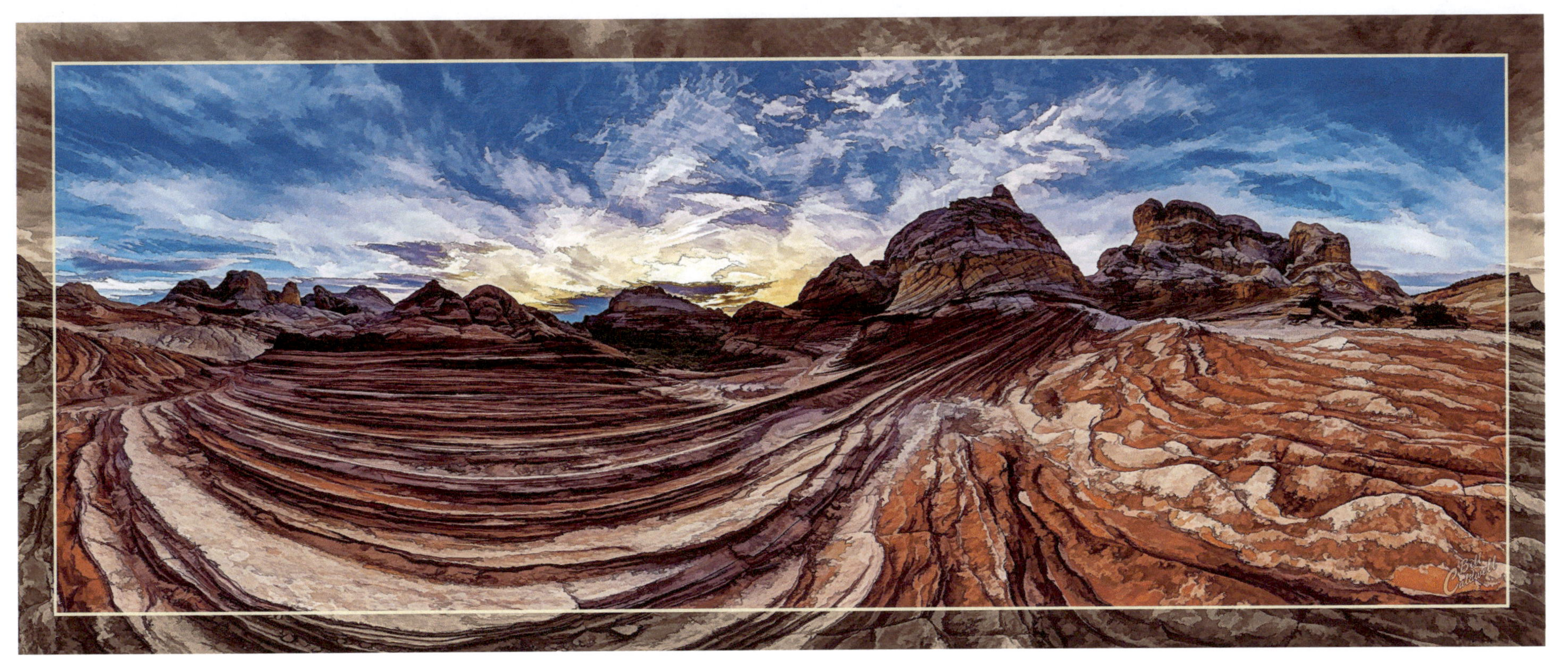

There I Travel…

"For me there is only the traveling on paths that have heart, on any path that may have heart. There I travel, and the only worthwhile challenge is to traverse its full length. And there I travel, looking, looking, breathlessly." — don Juan Matus (via Carlos Castaneda)

By the time I graduated high school in 1974, I knew I had to pursue my love of photography in college. Although I wasn't at all sure how I was going to pay for it, I knew this was a "path with a heart." With my good grades and a glowing recommendation letter from my favorite high school teacher, I was accepted at one of the best photography colleges at that time, Brooks Institute - School of Photographic Art and Science. With my dad's help and the money I made working at a convenience store during high school, I was able to buy the camera equipment that I would need at the school. We couldn't afford the tuition, so I applied for a federally guaranteed student loan through one of the local banks and this paid for my tuition. I also got a job at a fast food restaurant so I was able to help pay for my living expenses. Now all I needed was a place to live. We found a small inexpensive trailer park located near the edge of town. Somebody just happened to be selling a very old, very inexpensive 24 foot travel trailer which my dad bought for me. I was able to build a very small darkroom in the back end of the trailer, and although it was a tight little living space, it filled my needs and it was very inexpensive to live there. The bad thing about this trailer park was that it was located right next to the railroad tracks. Sometimes, in the middle of the night, a freight train would come roaring down the tracks and the whole trailer would vibrate and shake. The noise was so loud I thought the train was going to come right through my trailer! So it wasn't what you'd call the ideal situation, but everything lined up so I was able to pursue my dream of photography.

Looking back on it now, I realize that at that time, it never occurred to me that I might not be able to pursue my dream—that thought never entered my mind. I knew that it wouldn't be easy, I knew that I would have to work hard for it, and I think some part of me knew that somehow it would work out. I was accepted by a pretty exclusive school, I procured a student loan, I was able to buy the necessary camera equipment, I picked up a really cheap old car that was in fairly good running condition, I found an inexpensive place to live where I could have my own darkroom, and I had a part time job so I could help pay my way. I truly believe now that the Universe was helping to pave the way so I could follow this "path with a heart."

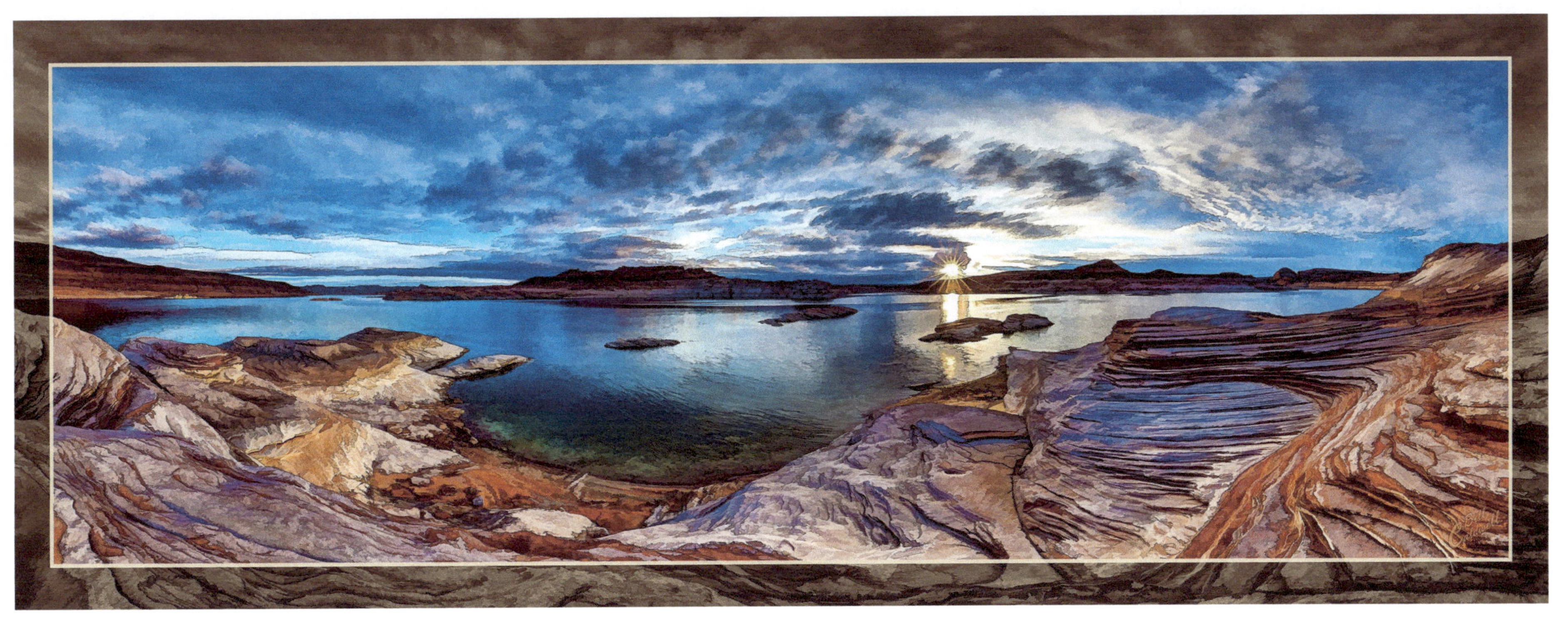

Sacred Rising

"I learned this, at least, by my experiment; that if one advances confidently in the direction of his dreams, and endeavors to live the life which he has imagined, he will meet with a success unexpected in common hours.." — Henry David Thoreau

One day when I was going to college, I didn't have any classes until later in the day, so I decided to go surfing early in the morning. By then I had been surfing on a regular basis for about eight years so I had lots of experience, and surfing had become second nature to me. On this particular day, I had gone to a surfing spot that had a lot of sharp rocks and boulders lining the shore and the bottom. As I was paddling out, a wave popped up in front of me and as usual I pushed the nose of my board down and ducked under it. I had done this hundreds of times in the past with no problems. What happened next completely shocked me. The wave didn't seem to be very big and yet it hit me with such force and violence that it ripped my surfboard right out of my hands, knocked the air out of my lungs, and jammed my body, head first, down into the bottom. The first amazing thing is that at that particular spot my head hit a small patch of sand instead of rocks. If my head had hit the rocks instead of the sand I would've been knocked unconscious and then drowned. It was early in the morning and I was the only person on this entire beach so there was nobody there to rescue me. The second amazing thing is that I didn't break my neck. The force and violence of this event astonished me because the wave just didn't seem to be that big. After hitting the bottom, I was thrashed around for what seemed like an eternity, so by the time I got back up to the surface I was gasping for breath. I felt like I just went through the agitation cycle in a washing machine. I made it back to the shoreline and I sat there for a while, stunned and amazed that I didn't break my neck or drown. This was another instance when I felt like I had been saved by some sort of divine intervention, and reinforced my sense of awe and wonder, and the feeling that there is more going on in the world than meets the eye. I now believe that one of my spirit guides protected me from serious injury.

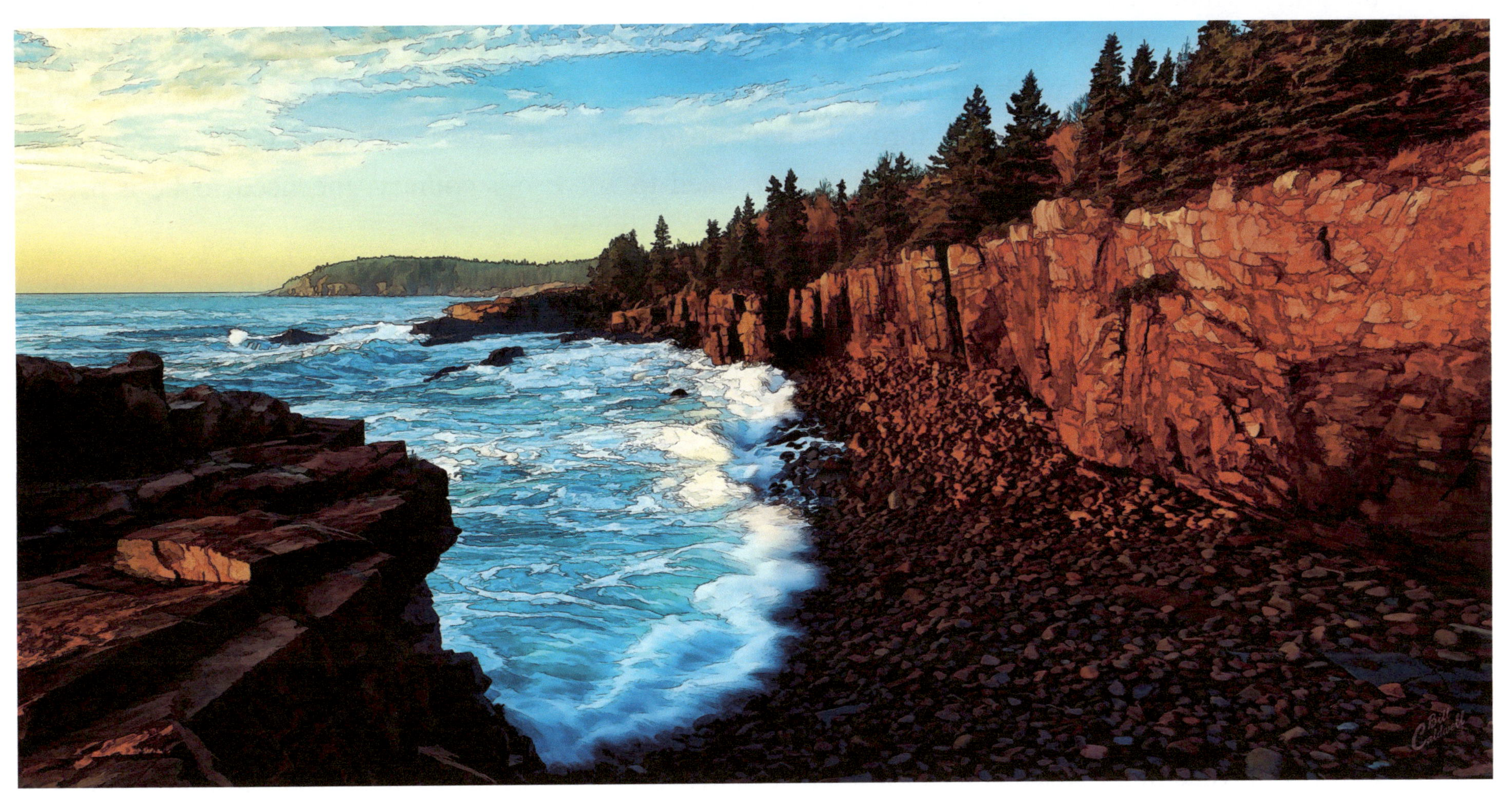

Ocean Energy

Although it may not seem that way at times, we are never alone. We are all connected metaphysically through an unseen network of energy. We all come into this world connected with Source Energy, our spirit guides, teachers, and our higher self (the greater part of Who-You-Really-Are).

By the time I graduated college, I realized that I was a lot more interested in the *art* of photography than the *business* of photography. So, to make a living, I went to work with my dad and brother in residential construction. I did construction work for a few years and although I had a great sense of satisfaction doing that work, seeing the fruits of my labor in the form of a house being built, there was still something missing. I felt this need to serve the greater good in some way, the need to serve my country, the need to be a part of something greater than myself and to do more than just make a living.

My dad was an aeronautical engineer for many years and I had a great love for airplanes and aviation. I also wanted to serve my country, so I joined the U.S. Air Force. Doing this took a great leap of faith on my part. Flying military aircraft is inherently dangerous after all, and the thought of being involved in some future war was frightening to say the least. So I had this trepidation, but I knew in my heart that this was what I wanted to do. It wasn't until I had completed Undergraduate Navigator Training that I found out I was being selected for Combat Search and Rescue (CSAR). I was so elated I had goosebumps! CSAR was only offered occasionally to graduating navigators because there are so few CSAR aircraft in the USAF. That's when I knew, beyond the shadow of doubt, that this was what I was meant to do at this stage of my life, that this was "a path with a heart."

I spent 20 years in the Air Force so there's lots of stories I could tell about my experiences, but that's not what this book is about. The significant thing is that the decision to join the Air Force was a huge crossroads in my life and had far reaching consequences for the rest of my life. Soon after I joined the Air Force, because of my changed circumstances, I met my wife and we've been married for 34 years now. While I was in the Air Force, and after I retired, I continued reading various books and magazines about spirituality, science, and photography. I also continued practicing my photography, and went hiking and exploring with my wife whenever we had the chance. After I retired from the Air Force, I worked in construction for several years until I injured my lower back. Since then I've been working full time on my artistic photography.

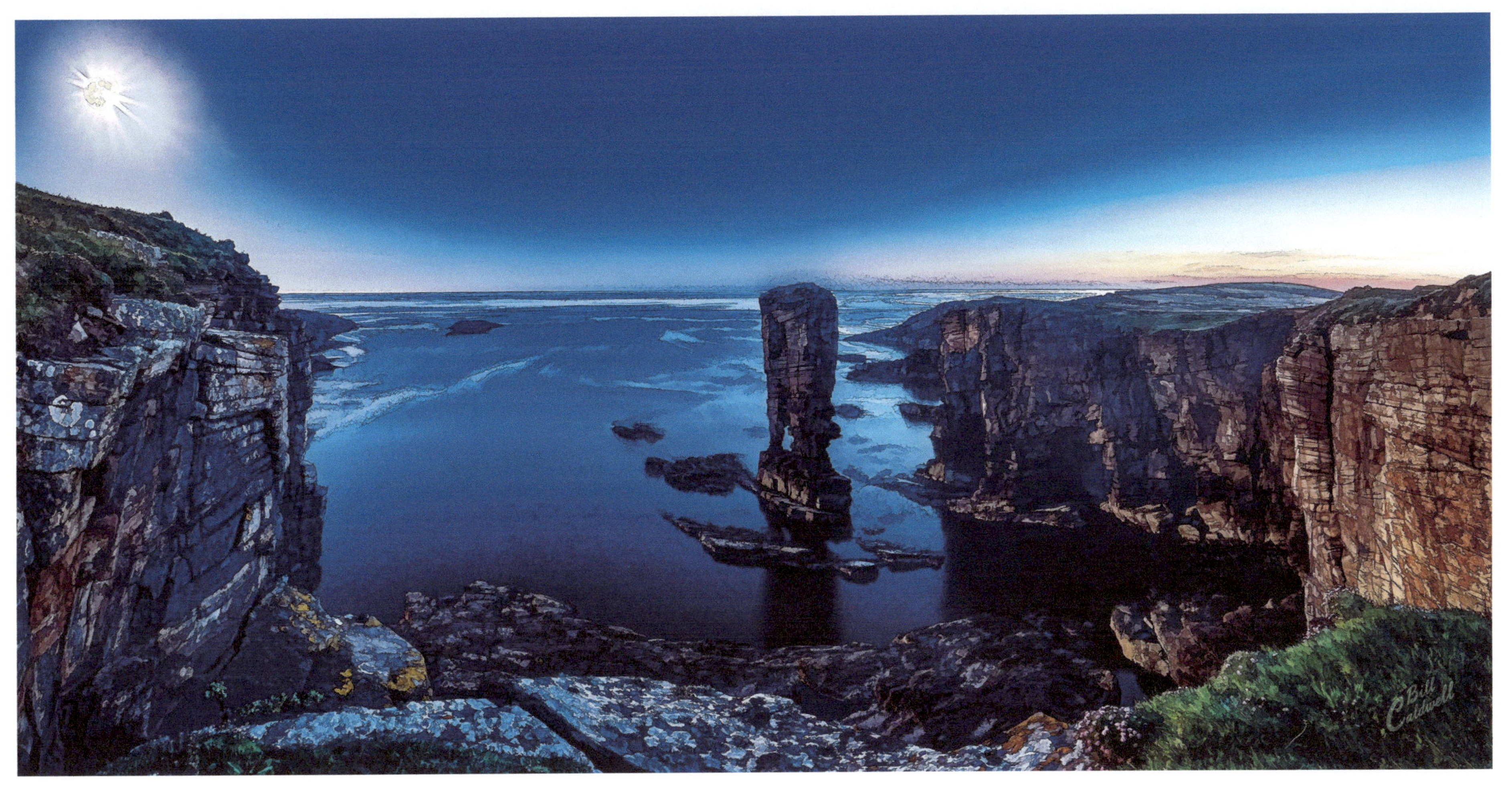

The Time Between

Does your spirit wander in the time between? The time between day and night, sleeping and waking, living and passing, the time between lives. Where does your spirit take you? Do you travel to distant planets, distant galaxies, new dimensions? Where do you go in the time between?

PART 2

What I've Learned & What I Believe

If there's anything I've learned during my life, it's that there is much more going on in the world and the universe than meets the eye. Much more going on than our five senses or scientific instruments will show you, much more than any religion will tell you, much more than most people are aware of or can imagine. The universe is a fantastic and mysterious place—what many Native Americans call the Great Mystery. Ultimately, I believe that we are all connected, we are all one.

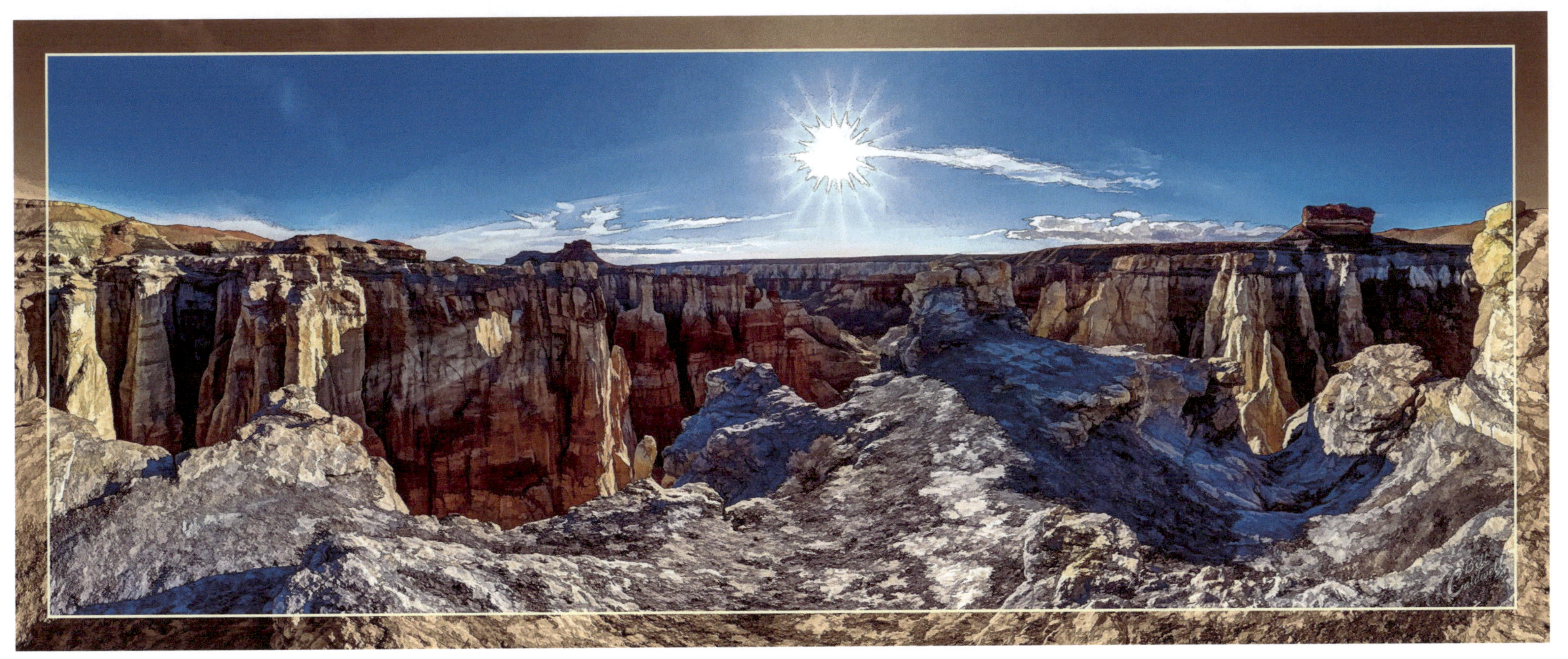

The Sentinel Kings

"From Wakan Tanka, the Great Spirit, there came a great unifying life force that flowed in and through all things—the flowers of the plains, blowing winds, rocks, trees, birds, animals—and was the same force that had been breathed into the first man. Thus all things were kindred, and were brought together by the same Great Mystery." — Chief Luther Standing Bear (Oglala Sioux)

Many people adopt whatever religious belief their parents and family subscribe to simply because that's the way they were raised. Some people reject their parents religion and go on to look for some other religion or they might reject all religions and all forms of spirituality. Still others simply go through the motions of going to church because that's what's expected and they want to fit in with the rest of their family and community. Although I was exposed to a certain type of Christian church when I was a young child, that ended shortly after my parents divorced. For the most part, I wasn't raised to believe in any particular religion or belief system. So when I was old enough to care about such things, I was free to explore whatever religion or spiritual beliefs I wanted to. When I was in junior high school I started reading books about spirituality and philosophy and I've continued that curiosity throughout my life. I don't believe any single book, religion, or spiritual teacher has all the answers. I believe that it is up to each individual to explore what's available and to look within themselves to find their own spiritual path—to find their own spiritual truth, the truth that resonates with their heart and soul.

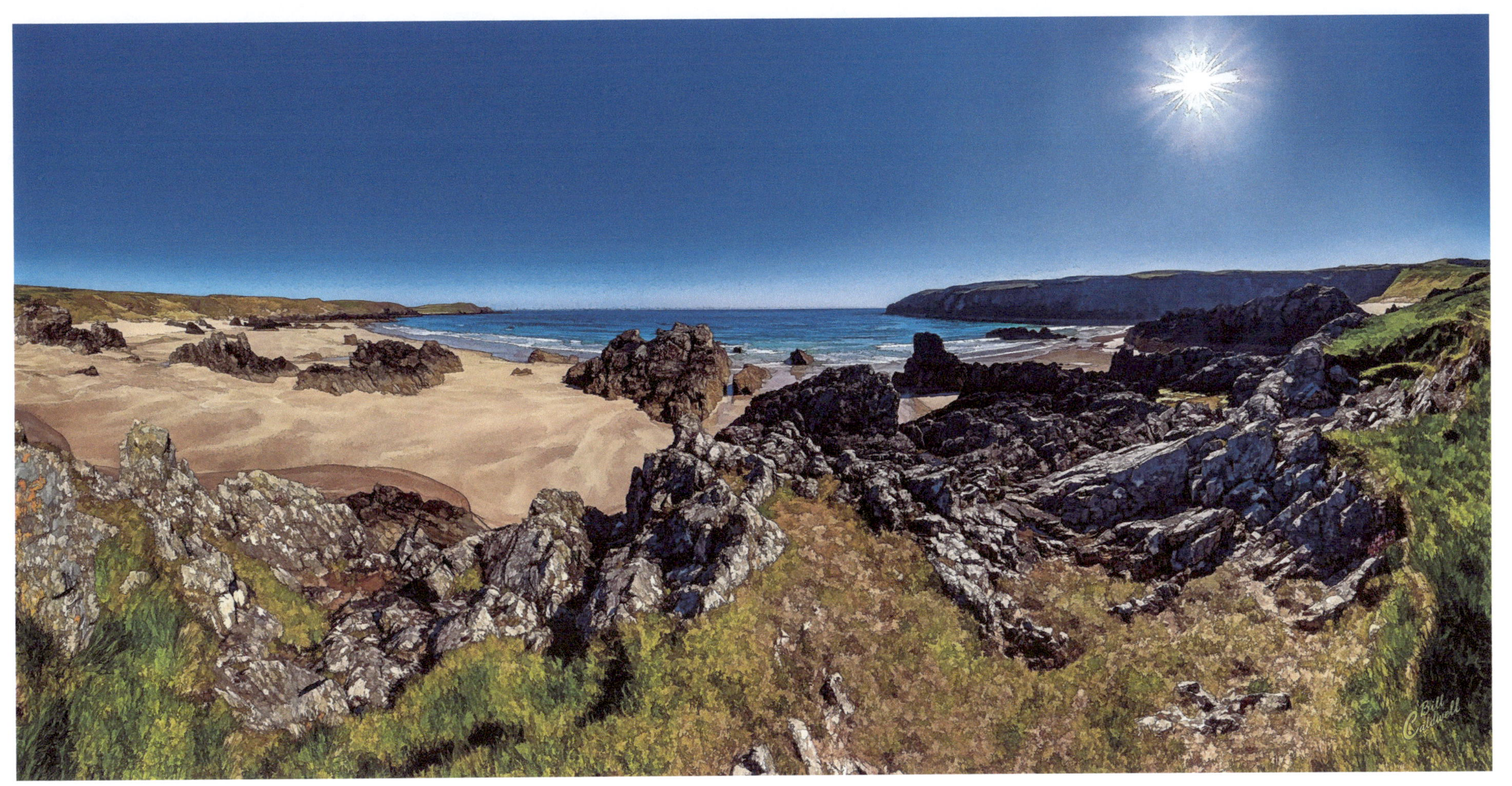

Finding Your Way

We are all on a spiritual journey of learning, growth, and expansion, whether we're conscious of it or not. There are many paths we can take and we all have our own pathway.

Spirituality

*"Being spiritual has nothing to do with what you believe and everything
to do with your state of consciousness."*   — *Eckhart Tolle*

You don't have to be a monk, a nun, or a priest to be spiritual, and you don't have to go to church either. Religion is just one of the many spiritual pathways you can follow. And you don't have to be a hermit living in a cave or renounce all of your worldly possessions—the physical world is a manifestation of spirit and, while we are here, we cannot separate ourselves from the physical. For me, being spiritual is about waking up and living your life consciously. Being spiritual is about seeking the truth—the truth about why we are all here, the truth about who you really are, and recognizing the truth and dysfunctionality of your own ego. Being spiritual is about living life with a reverence for all life. Being spiritual is about coming into alignment with your higher self or soul, what Abraham-Hicks refers to as the greater part of Who-You-Really-Are.

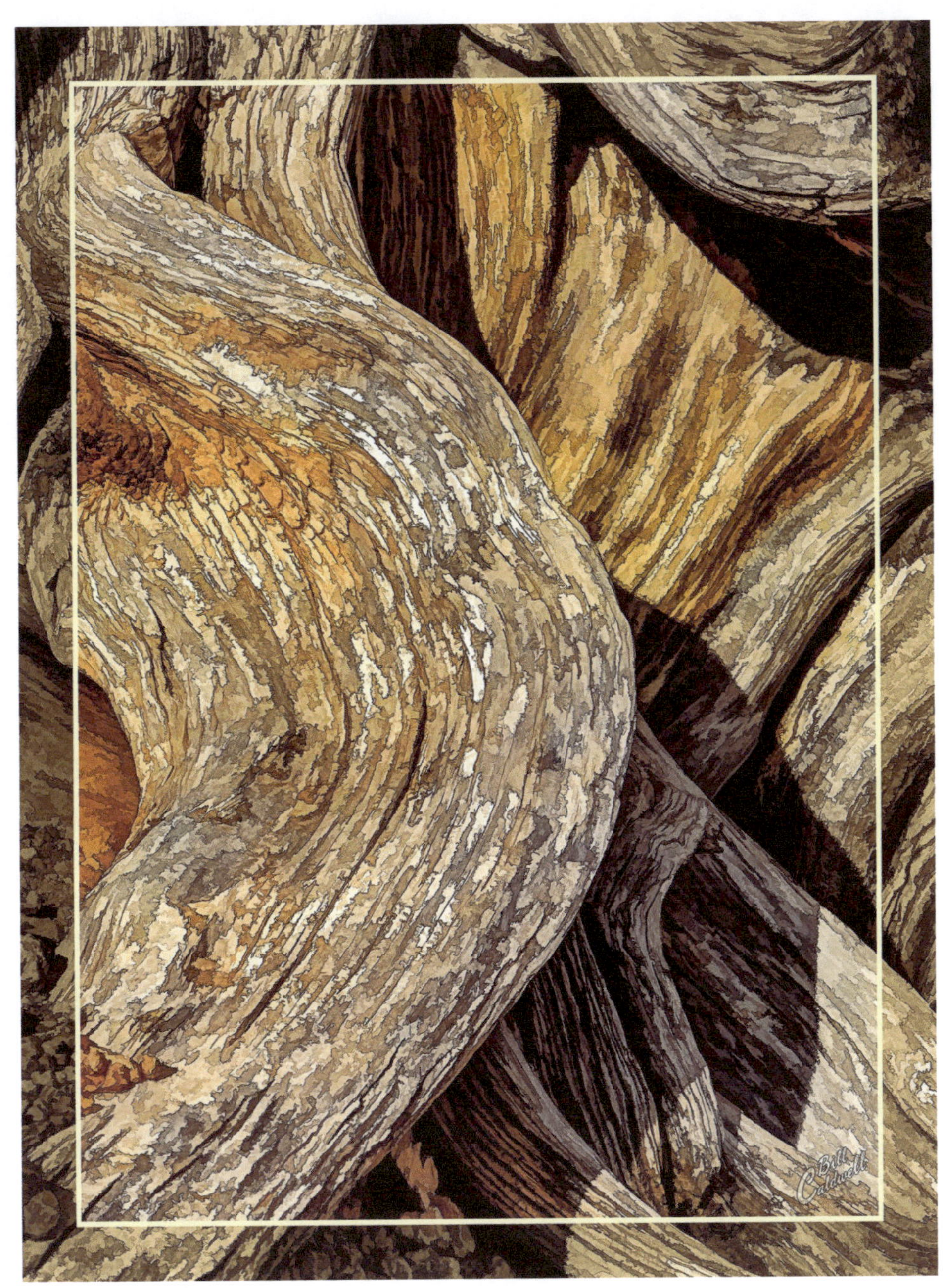

True Growth

"As we become aware of our spiritual nature, we recognize our true essence. We are immortal and divine. Renouncing violence, hate, dominance, selfishness, and ownership of people and things becomes even easier with this recognition. Accepting love, compassion, charity, hope, faith, and cooperation becomes the natural thing to do." — Dr. Brian Weiss

My first encounters with organized religion came when I was a young child. I vaguely remember going to church on Sundays when I was very young. When I was still quite young, my family moved to California and we stopped going to church. A few years later my parents got divorced, and after a short time living with my biological mother, my siblings and I moved in with my dad and stepmom, Chris. Sometimes when we would visit Chris's parents I would overhear their conversations about metaphysics. I think these experiences planted the seed of my curiosity about religion, metaphysics, and spirituality. As a teenager, many of the sci-fi books I read addressed religion and spirituality in interesting ways and gave me a lot of food for thought. Later, when I was going to college, I read the King James version of the Bible from cover to cover—a daunting task that took quite a bit of self-discipline to complete! I also tried going to different church services with various friends, but those experiences never resonated with me. The one thing that has resonated with me throughout my life is being outdoors and experiencing nature, whether it's the beach and the ocean, or the mountains and canyons. I've come to realize that connecting with the natural world is an important part of my spirituality and my general well-being.

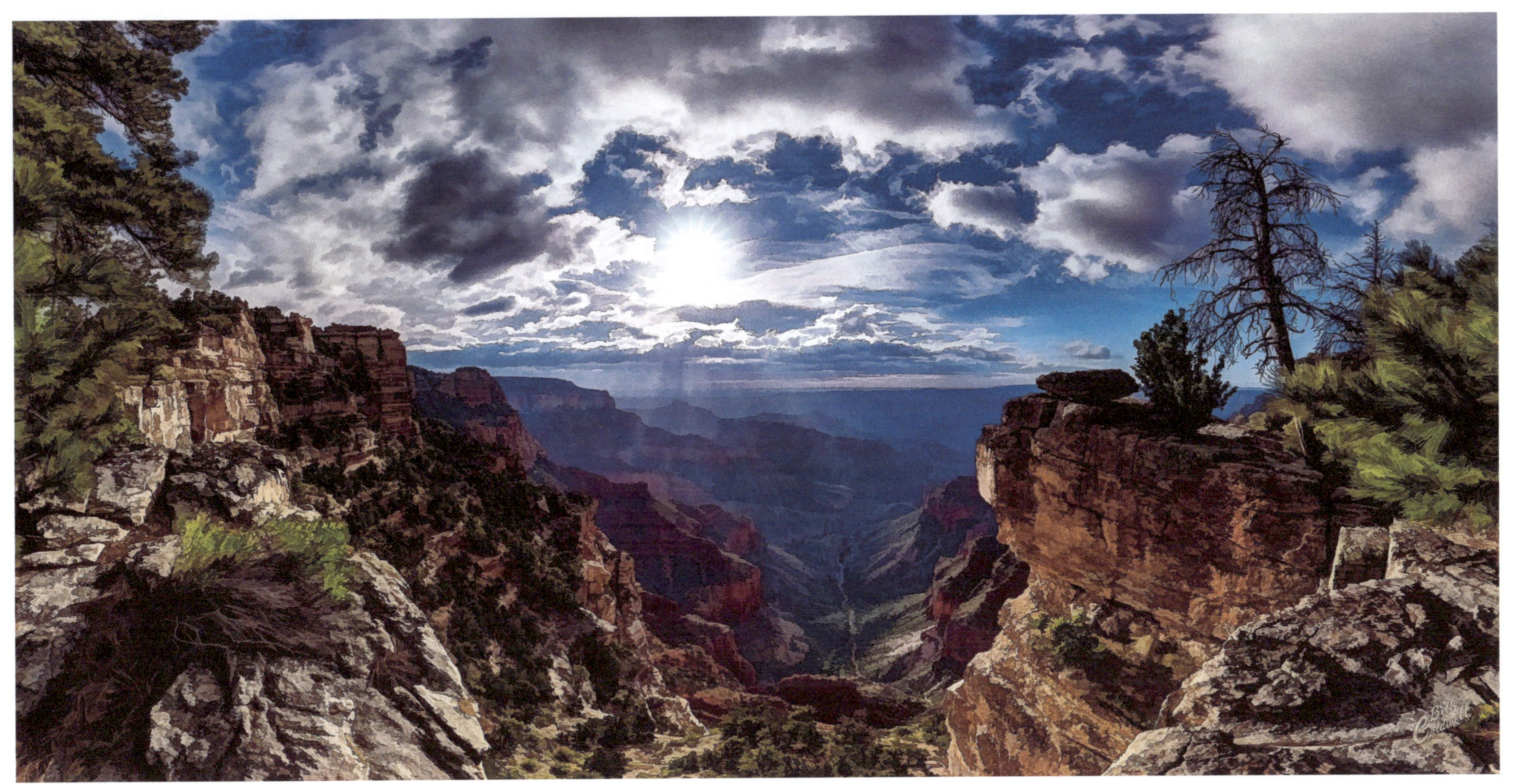

Where the Ancients Gathered

"Nonphysical is not asking you to ascribe to some specific label or stand in specific corners or in specific synagogues or churches with specific words. You are beings who are blessed and who are deserving of Well-being, and you will find your Well-being in many different ways—and the labels simply do not matter." — Abraham-Hicks

For me, being outside in nature's beauty is like being in a different kind of church—a church created by the natural forces of the universe. One of the definitions of the word sacred is "worthy of or regarded with reverence, awe, or respect." In this sense, I consider these beautiful natural places as sacred ground. When I'm standing in nature, taking pictures of these beautiful scenes, I have this feeling of awe and wonder. Just as I felt when I took this next picture. The wind had died down to nothing so the water was glassy smooth and it was so very quiet and serene. The sun had set so the air was cooling down and there was such a sense of stillness. After I took my last picture I just stood there soaking in the feeling of beauty and stillness. And as I stood there at the edge of the lake, an otter went swimming by only a few feet from where I was standing, something I had never seen before. I had such a feeling of awe and wonder, truly a spiritual experience. So you might want to try sitting in nature. Just sit in silence and soak in the beauty and serenity.

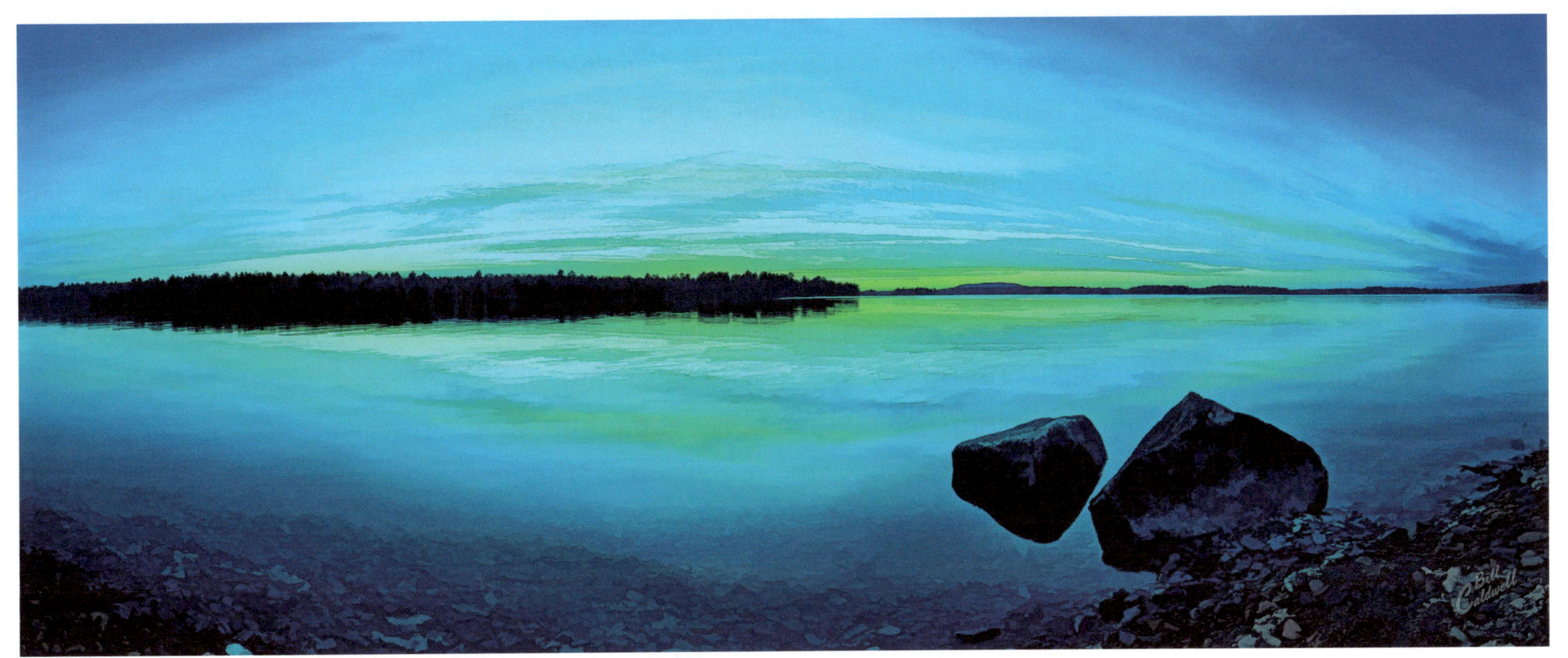

Reflections of Serenity

"Silence is essential. We need silence, just as much as we need air, just as much as plants need light. If our minds are crowded with words and thoughts, there is no space for us." — Thich Nhat Hanh

Meditation

"The internal dialogue is what grounds people in the daily world. The world is such and such or so and so, only because we talk to ourselves about its being such and such and so and so. The passageway into the world of shamans opens up after the warrior has learned to shut off his internal dialogue"
— don Juan Matus (via Carlos Castaneda)

The first time I learned about meditation I was in high school taking a class called General Semantics. The teacher had us practice a simple form of meditation where we just sat in our seats quietly and focused on relaxing the muscles of the shoulders and neck. Around that same time there was a very popular book about Transcendental Meditation by the Indian guru Maharishi Mahesh Yogi. At first, meditation seemed like something esoteric—something that only gurus or monks would practice. In time, I began to realize that there's nothing mysterious about meditation. Meditation is not something that is reserved for yogis or gurus or monks. In it's most basic form, meditation is simply the practice of sitting quietly in stillness and letting go of the continuous internal dialogue that goes on in our minds. This helps to relieve physical and mental tension and helps us to connect with our higher self/Source Energy. Meditation has many benefits and there's a lot of different ways to go about doing it. More recently I took a meditation class with Sarah McLean. She has studied many meditation techniques across the world and identified several basic commonalities, and I found her class to be very helpful. There is no single right way of doing it, so find the way that works best for you. You don't have to be sitting in the classic lotus position and you don't have to be in a particular location like an ashram or monastery either. You could be sitting in your living room, your car (parked of course), your office, sitting outside in nature, or in a museum looking at a painting. In fact, as you become more proficient at meditating, you can simply gaze at a beautiful picture, in a state of mental stillness, and connect with the beauty and energy of that place.

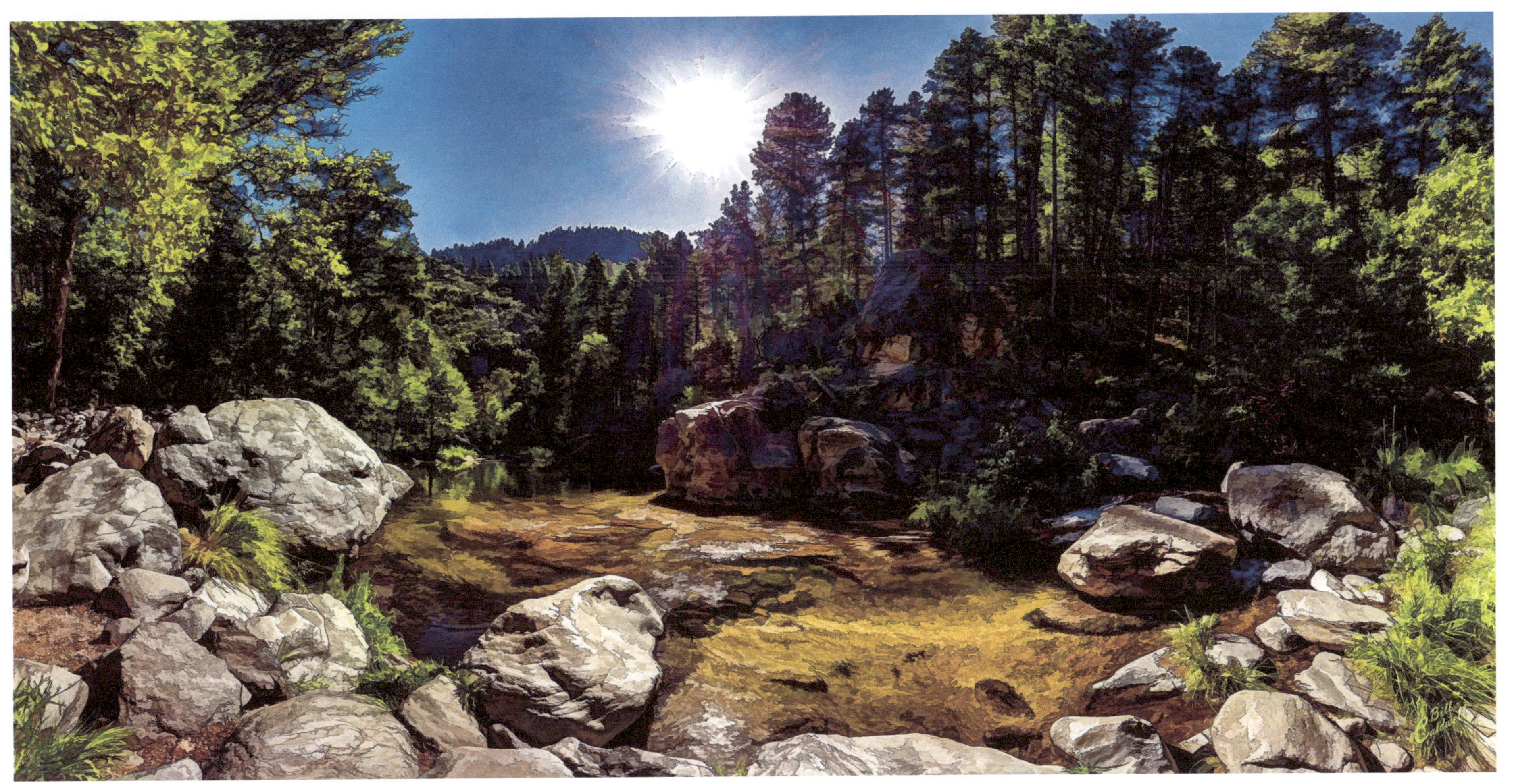

The Meditation Pond

"When we dance, the journey itself is the point, as when we play music, the playing itself is the point. And exactly the same thing is true in meditation. Meditation is the discovery that the point of life is always arrived at in the immediate moment." — Alan Watts

There's a funny scene in the movie "Eat Pray Love" where Julia Roberts is sitting in an Indian ashram meditating for the first time. She looks at the clock and starts meditating, for what seems like a very long time. But when she looks at the clock again, only a single minute has passed by! I felt the same way the first few times that I tried meditation, but the more I practiced the easier it became and the deeper I went.

"Yoga is a method for restraining the natural turbulence of thoughts, which otherwise impartially prevent all men, of all lands, from glimpsing their true nature of Spirit. Yoga cannot know a barrier of East and West any more than does the healing and equitable light of the sun." — Paramahansa Yogananda

Many people find it beneficial to practice a form of meditation-in-motion like Tai Chi or Yoga. Although I didn't know it at the time, surfing became a very powerful form of meditation-in-motion when I was a young man. It's hard to put into words the feeling that I had when I was surfing. The more experienced I became, the more effortless it became so I was able to just go with the flow of the wave. There were times when I would feel so completely connected with the energy of the wave that I would forget that I was separate from my board and separate from the wave. It felt as if I had become an integral part of that beautiful flowing energy; a truly transcendental, spiritual experience. When you're practicing tai chi or surfing or many other activities, you become very focused on the present moment—an important part of meditation.

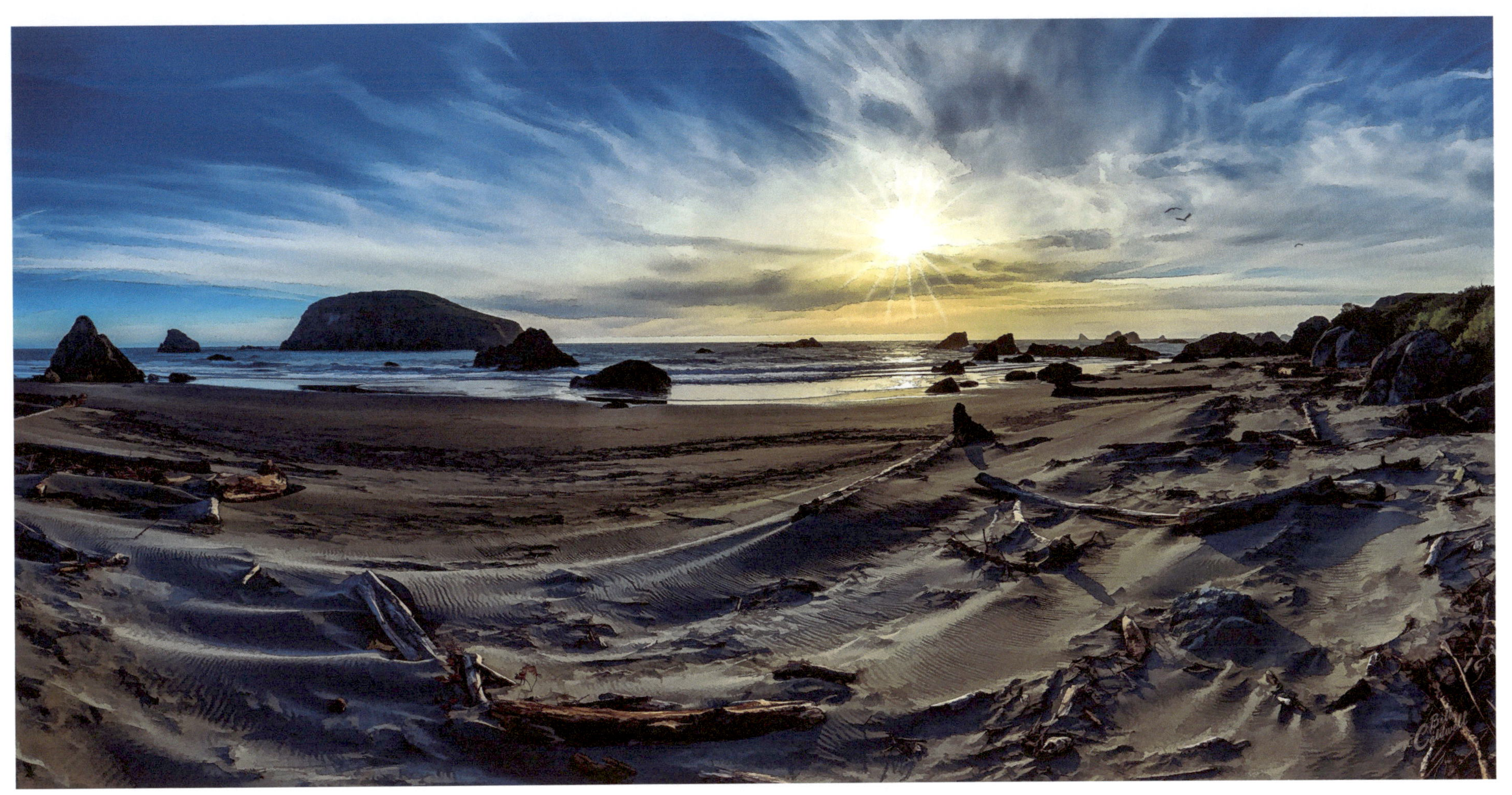

In the Beginning

"Nothing ever happened in the past; it happened in the Now. Nothing will ever happen in the future; it will happen in the Now. Realize deeply that the present moment is all you have. Make the Now the primary focus of your life." — Eckhart Tolle

Years later, my wife and I tried listening to guided meditation CDs and this worked very well for us. Listening to the words helped to turn off that internal dialogue so we could enter a deeper state of meditation. As we continued to practice, it became easier to reach that state of internal stillness. Recently we started listening to soft music (with no words) while holding a polished sphere of blue apatite stone and that works nicely for us. Being outside in a natural setting, connecting with the beauty of nature is also very effective. I love sitting by a stream or river and listening to the water flowing over the rocks, or sitting by the ocean and listening to the waves crashing. There's a movement of energy that you can feel deep inside. As you become more proficient, you can reach a deeper state of consciousness and internal stillness. Sometimes, as I get deeper in my state of meditation, the outside world seems to disappear. I no longer hear the music or my breathing or other external sounds. It's as if my mind and spirit have been transported to a different space or dimension. Sometimes, in these moments of deep meditation, my spirit guides or other nonphysical beings take me to other places—other planets, other galaxies, other dimensions (a form of astral travel). This is always done for the purpose of spiritual growth and expansion.

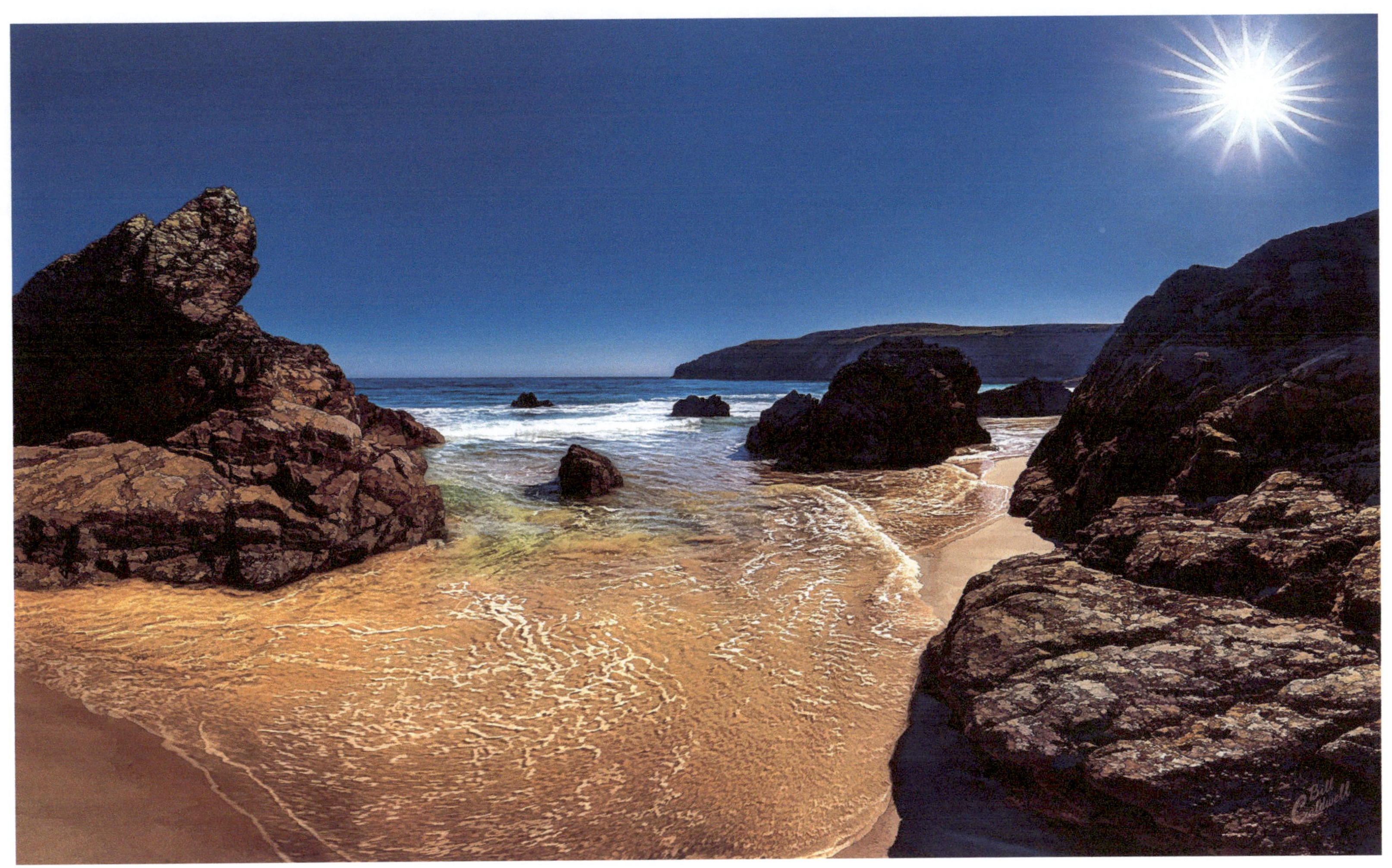

The Movement of Energy

Sit in nature and be present in stillness.
Sit by a stream or a river and listen to the water flowing.
Sit by the seashore and listen to the waves.
There's a movement of energy that you can feel deep inside.

Finding Your Center

Many books and teachers talk about "finding your center" (or center of balance). What does this mean? Teachers like Abraham-Hicks and Eckhart Tolle talk about finding a balance between your feelings (or intuition), and your thinking mind. If we rely solely on our thinking mind we can get off on all kinds of tangents. In his book "Heart of the Soul," Gary Zukav tells the story of when his uncle, a Native American, once told him "The hardest journey a person will ever make is from here to here," pointing from his head to his heart. It seems that many of us have a tendency to live mostly in our heads, relying mainly on our intellect and ignoring our feelings. I think it's important to note here that we are talking about heartfelt feelings—not egoic emotions. In his book "A New Earth—Awakening to Your Life's Purpose," Eckhart Tolle makes the distinction, and explains the difference, between feelings and egoic emotions like fear, anger, and jealousy.

For me, finding your center also means finding and exercising your connection with Source, your higher self, or soul. In the course of our physical lives, our connection to Source often gets pinched off or diminished by traumatic experiences and the unenlightened teachings of the people around us. So we have to find ways to open up and maintain that connection. Intuition is an important part of that connection and sometimes it can get drowned out by the hustle and bustle of what is going on around us, as well as our own thinking minds. I believe part of the spiritual journey we are all making here in the "Earth School" is learning to tune-in to and trust our intuition and deep feelings, and finding our centers of balance between listening to our hearts and listening to our intellects while navigating our pathways through life.

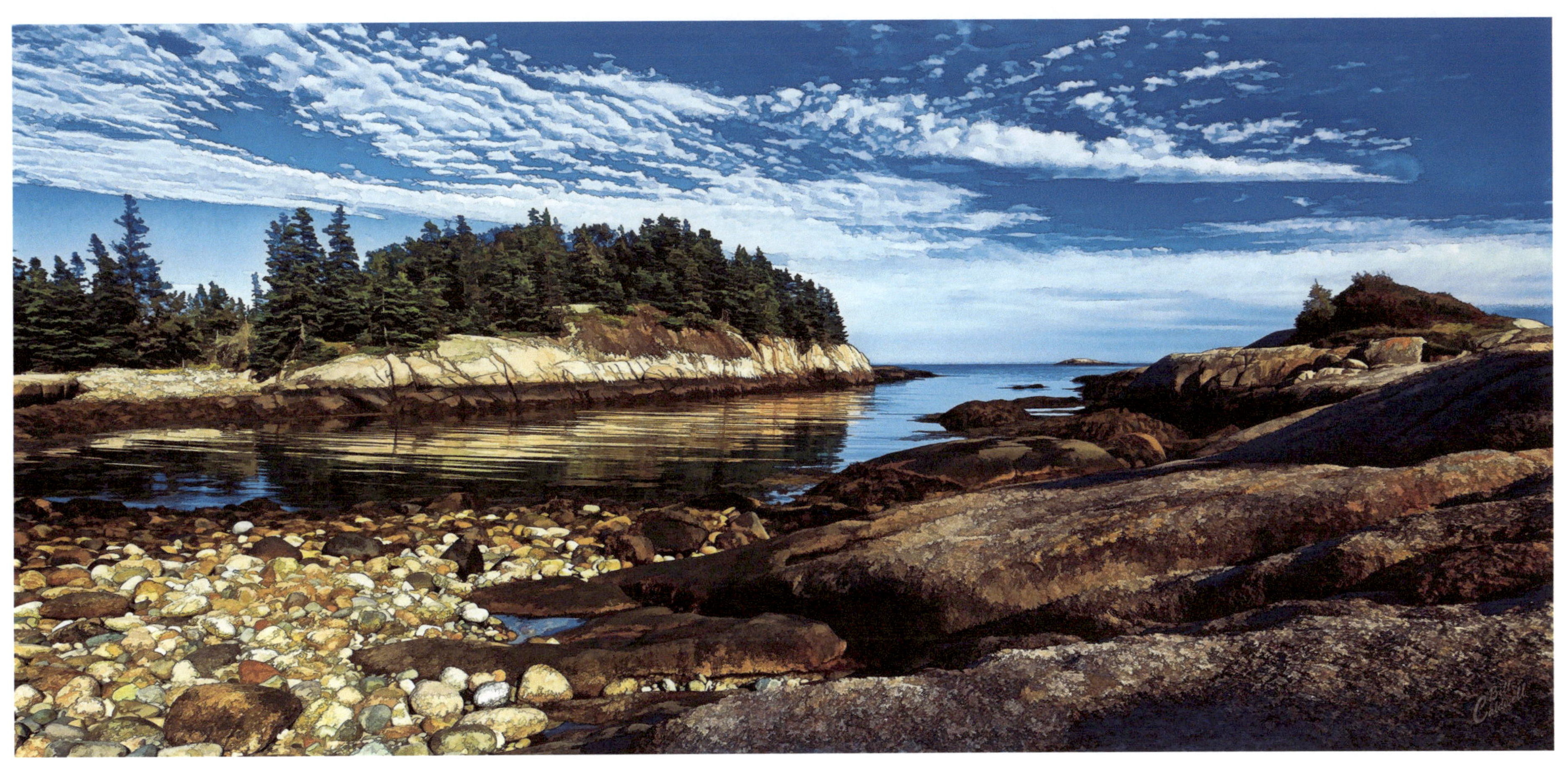

Trust Your Intuition

If you want to follow a deliberate spiritual path, listen to your heart.
Trust your intuition and trust what resonates with your soul.

Another way of looking at this comes from the ancient shamanic traditions of many cultures around the world. In his book "One Noble Truth," Clay Lomakayu writes about living in the center of your Circle, your Circle being the totality of who you are. He also writes about the importance of acknowledging every part of yourself, including the hurt emotions you may have rejected in the past. When we reject parts of ourselves, hurt feelings or aspects of ourselves that we don't like, we create an imbalance within. By acknowledging those rejected feelings and aspects of ourselves, and letting go of judgement, we can regain our center of balance.

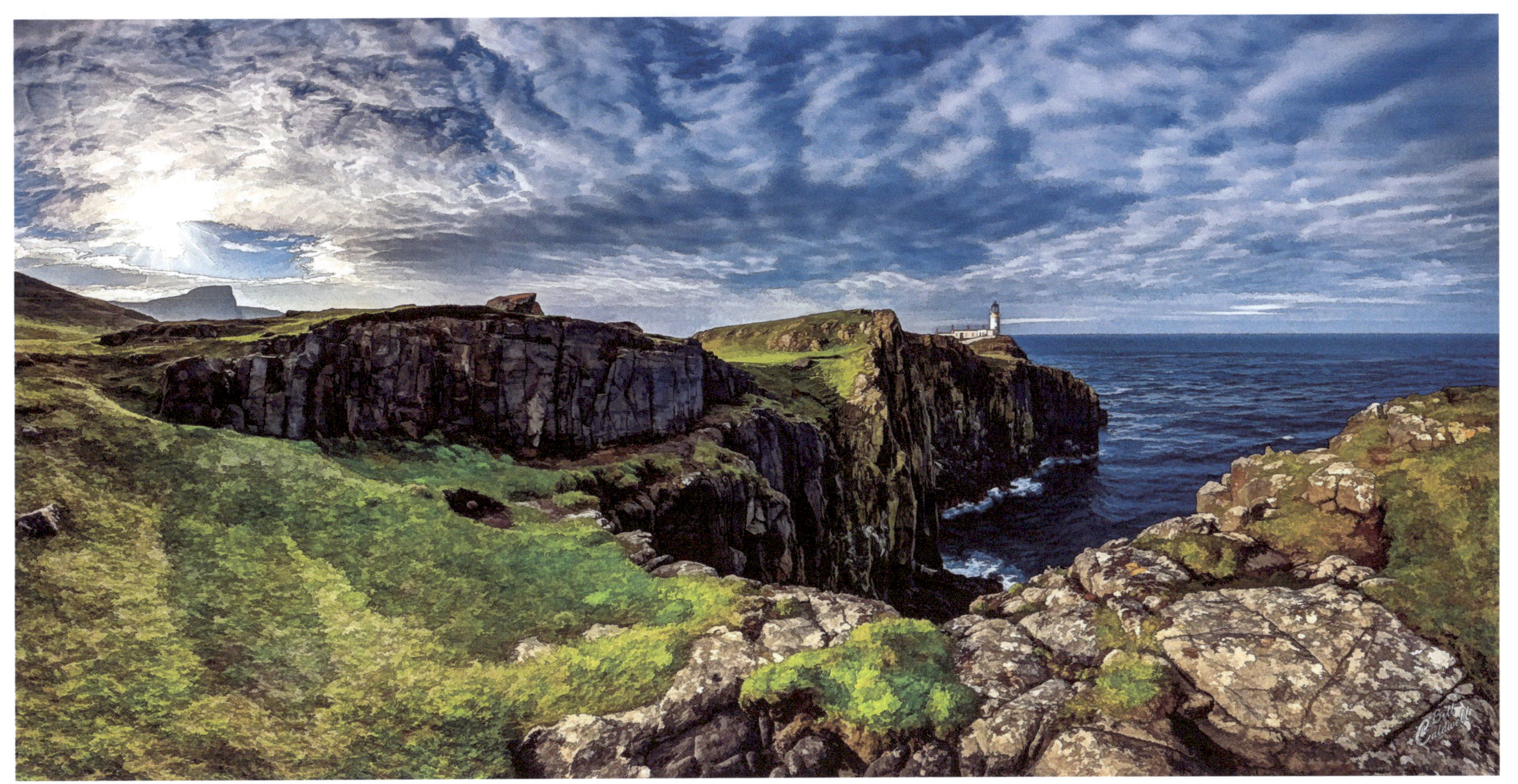

Coming Home

"If you have the feeling of having no center, like a ship adrift on the sea without the power to move or the inner compass to direct and guide, then finding your center is the journey of coming home to yourself."
— Clay Lomakayu

Choosing a Path

As we live our lives, we come across choices we have to make whether it involves our private life or our work life, like who to marry or which job to take. And each decision creates a new path to follow, along with feelings of uncertainty that may arise. But don't be afraid to make these decisions that come your way. If you try to connect with your higher self, you will be on the right path. If you feel like you haven't been able to connect with your higher self, don't worry—know that you're always receiving guidance even if you don't realize it. If you listen to your heart and trust your intuition, then follow through without fear, it will lead you to where you need to go.

I think we all want to find our purpose in life; something that makes us happy and is meaningful to our lives. I believe once this is found, it helps with our spiritual growth and expansion. The way you know this is the right path for you is in the joy of doing something that has meaning for you. Remember your early childhood, the things that made you happy—go in this direction. You will often find there's a progression leading you in a certain direction. My father was an aeronautical engineer and when I was young he would take us kids to airshows like the US Navy Blue Angels. I developed a love for airplanes and aviation and built many model airplanes. Later on, after college, I became very curious about the Vietnam war and what it was all about, so I read many books about that. A couple of the books talked about the combat search and rescue (CSAR) missions flown by the A-1 "Sandy" aircraft and the HC-130 "King" aircraft. These rescue stories struck a chord deep within me and a couple years later I joined the US Air Force and became a CSAR navigator in the HC-130 aircraft.

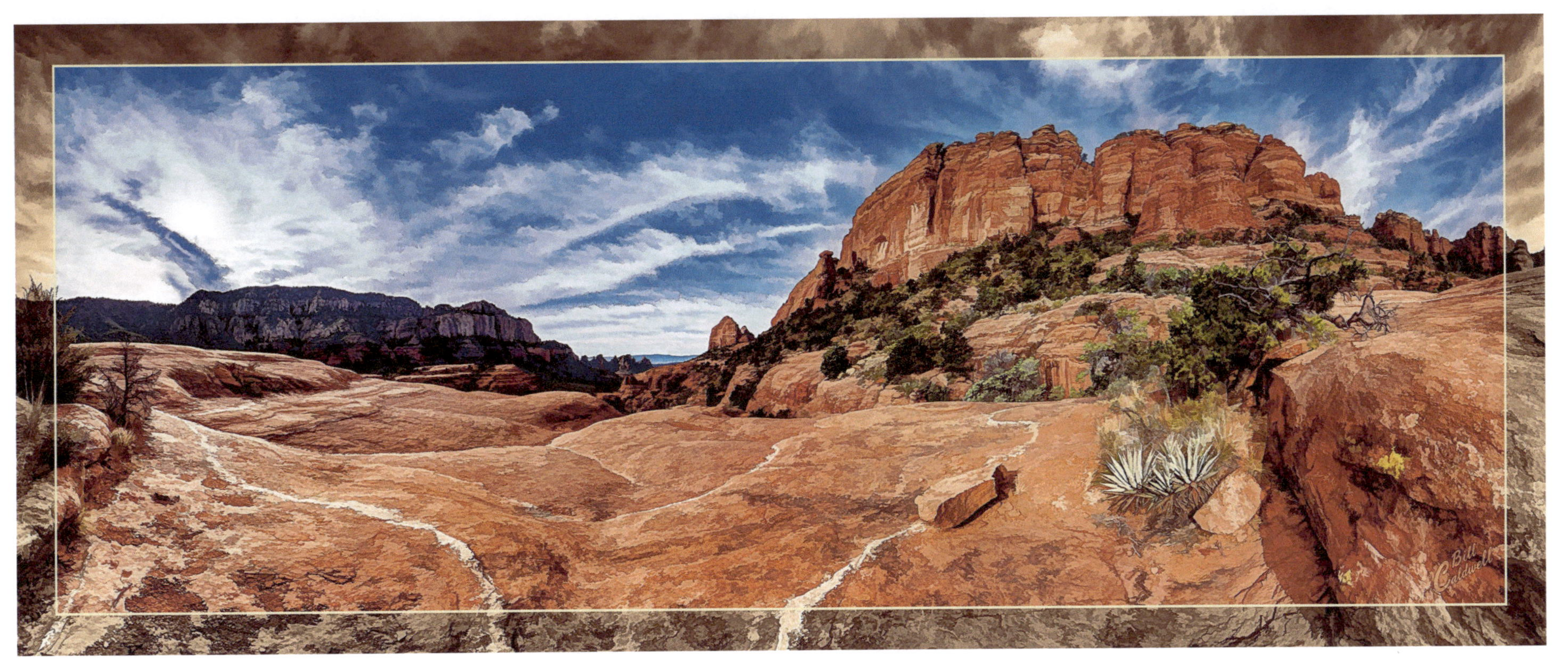

Choices

Whatever direction you choose will lead you to where you are supposed to be at that moment in time.

You may find that the Universe is sending you messages to help you along the way. As when I found those books about the Air Force CSAR missions. The Universe may also be steering you away from certain things. A friend of ours kept trying to go in a certain direction, but she kept running into obstacles and finally broke her ankle which forced her to reconsider what she was trying to do. So if you keep running into obstacles, that's probably not the direction you should be going.

Ultimately, the answer is that there is never a wrong path in life. No matter what direction you choose to take, it is the right path *at that time*. If, later on, that path no longer feels right to you, you can always change your direction. If you feel like you went off in the wrong direction and things happened that you thought should not have happened, know that *they were meant to happen*. As Eckhart Tolle said, "How do you know something is *supposed* to be happening? Because it *is* happening." Years later when you look back at the choices you made at the time, you will realize that you would not be where you are now. Whatever direction you choose will lead you to where you are supposed to be at that moment in time. There is no right or wrong choice to make. All roads lead you to where you are supposed to be at this time. So trust your intuition and listen to your heart—there you will find your answer.

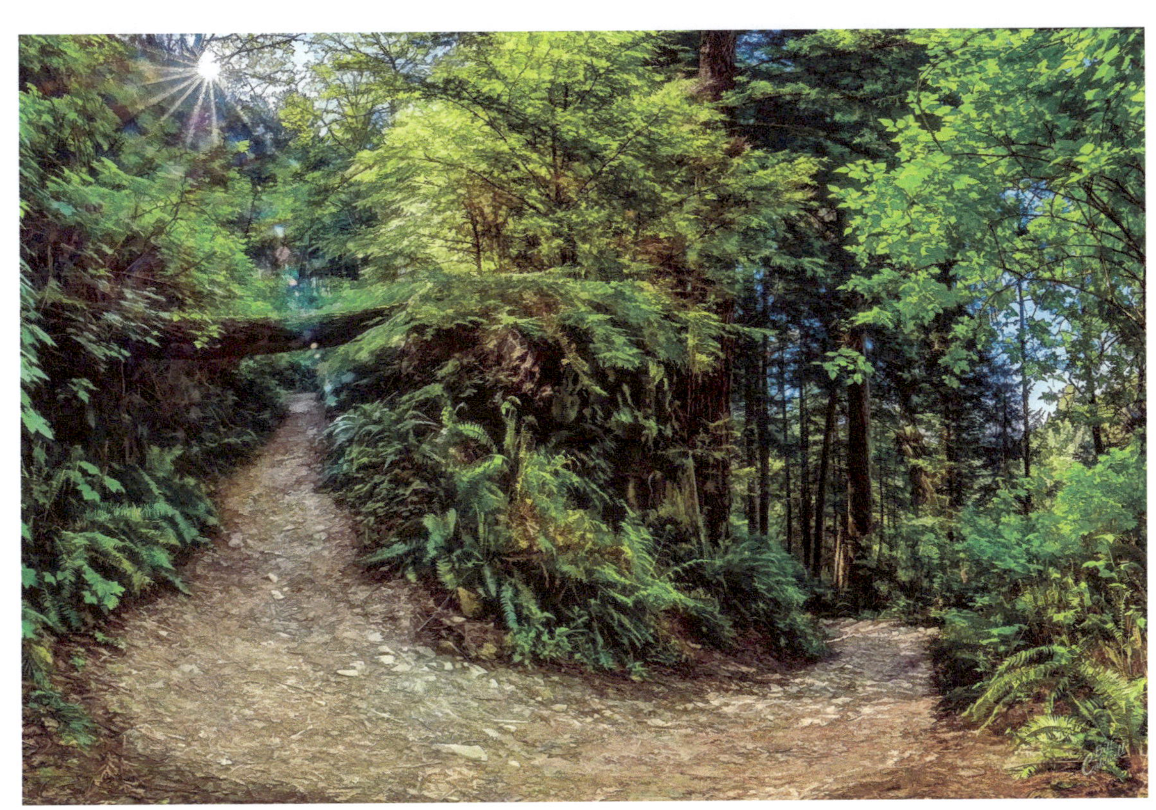

Walk Your Path

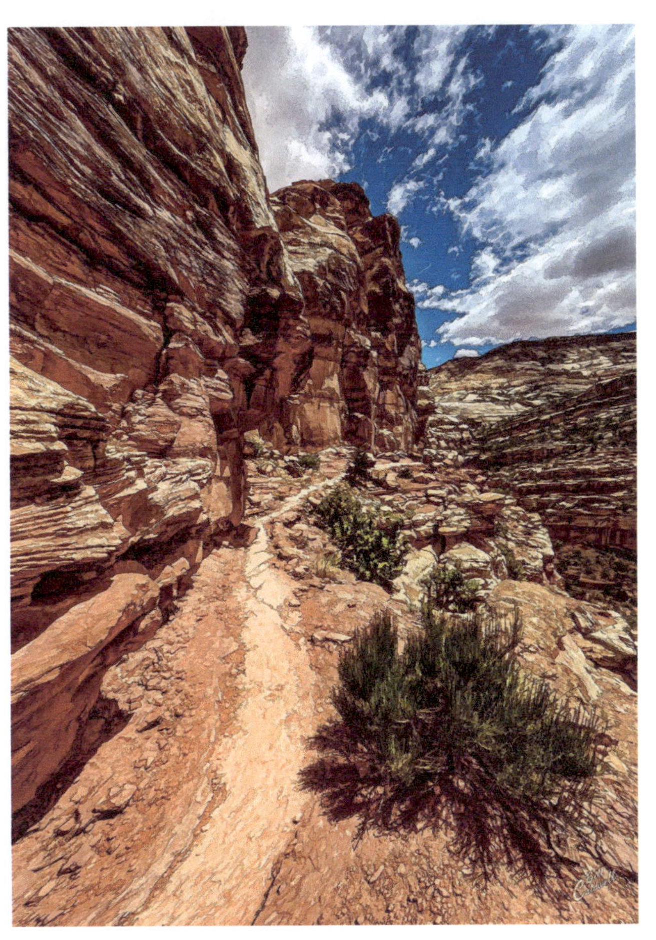

Follow Your Path

"The spiritual journey is individual, highly personal. It can't be organized or regulated. It isn't true that everyone should follow one path. Listen to your own truth." — Ram Dass

Harmony and Balance

One of the books I read when I was in high school is called "Seven Arrows" by Hyemeyohsts Storm. This is a beautiful book about the Plains Indian People and their culture, their philosophy, and their way of life. I felt a strong connection with the Native American way of life while I was reading this book. Many years later, while doing a past life regression meditation, I found out that I had at least one life as a Native American and I still feel that connection now. Part of the book is also the sad story of the passing of that way of life and I felt such a deep sorrow when I read those parts of the book. The Native American way of life was in tune with nature, in tune with the seasons, in tune with the land and with the animals. Most had a deep and abiding reverence for the land and for the natural world. They lived in harmony and balance with nature. The Navajo word for beauty, "nizhoni," also means harmony and balance.

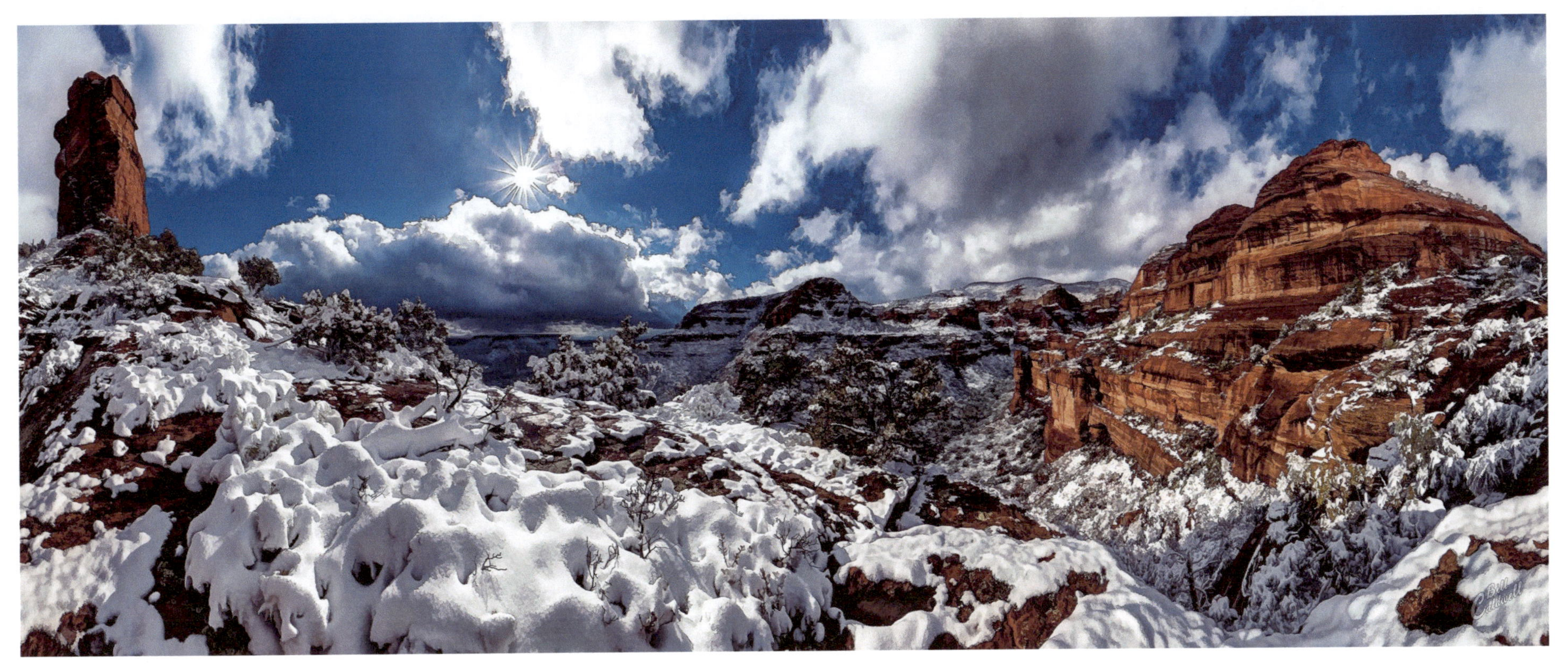

Blessings of Earth

When you walk in harmony and balance with nature, you can feel the beauty in your heart and soul.
You begin to feel a profound appreciation for nature's creations and the blessings of Earth.
In that present moment, you become one with all.

When you walk in harmony and balance with nature and the world around you, you can *feel* the beauty that surrounds you in a profound way. You can feel a connection with the land and the other living beings and you can feel your connection with Spirit and the Universe. You know that you're not alone, you know that you're not separate from the world. You can feel your existence, not as a mistake, not as random chance, but as an integral part of the Universe and you can feel the light of the Universe lighting your path. Living in harmony and balance with the natural world gives you a sense of connection with all life. You are in sync with the world, you are no longer in competition with the world. The Universe gives you what you need when you need it—life is no longer such a struggle for survival. Life becomes a dance, a continuous give and take where you are in cooperation with the world around you. This is also what life is like when you are in alignment with your higher self/soul, when you are in alignment with the greater part of Who-You-Really-Are.

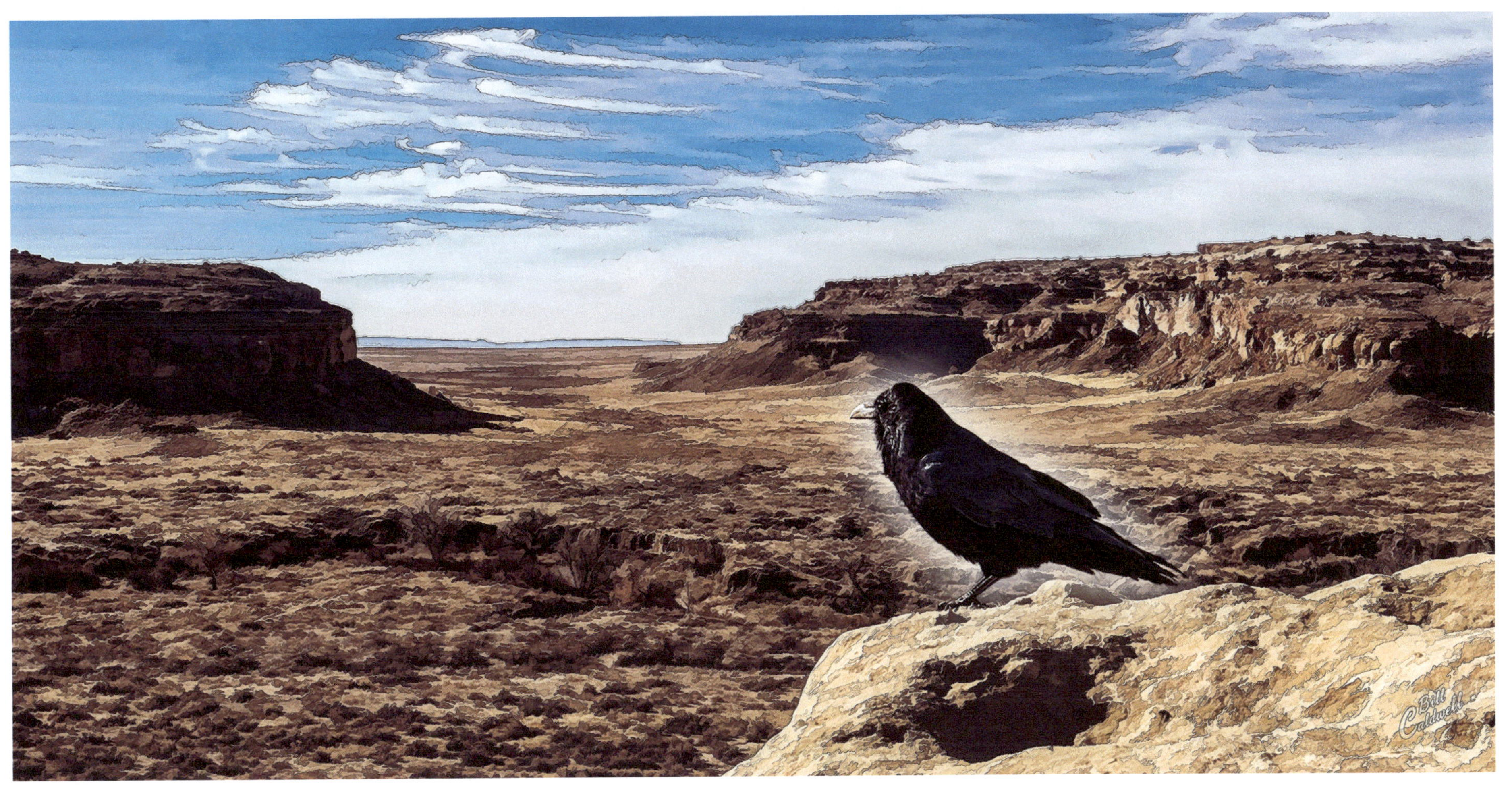

Walk in the Light

When you sit in stillness, you will begin to walk in harmony and balance—the Universe will light your path.

Connecting with Nature

I believe spending time in nature is just as important to the human spirit as food is to the body. I love spending time near the beautiful bodies of water—the oceans, lakes, and streams. I especially love the fascinating geologic formations of this planet and the beautiful trees. Trees were one of the first life forms and life as we know it here on planet Earth, would not exist without them. If you sit in stillness with one of these ancient beings, you can feel their presence. They are on this planet for our benefit and the benefit of all the beings that live on this planet.

"A forest is much more than what you see. And today I want to change the way you think about forests. You see, underground there is this other world, a world of infinite biological pathways that connect trees and allow them to communicate and allow the forest to behave as though it's a single organism. It might remind you of a sort of intelligence."   — Suzanne Simard

There is much more going on with the trees than most people are aware of or would have imagined. The trees that we see above the surface are just a small visible portion of a much larger, ancient living being. Researchers have discovered that trees communicate and cooperate with each other and even nurture each other. They have much to teach us if we can connect with them—if we're able to quiet our thinking minds and listen. Some people are already able to do this, although few would ever admit it for fear of being labeled a lunatic! Through meditation and practicing stillness we can connect with them and hear what they have to say.

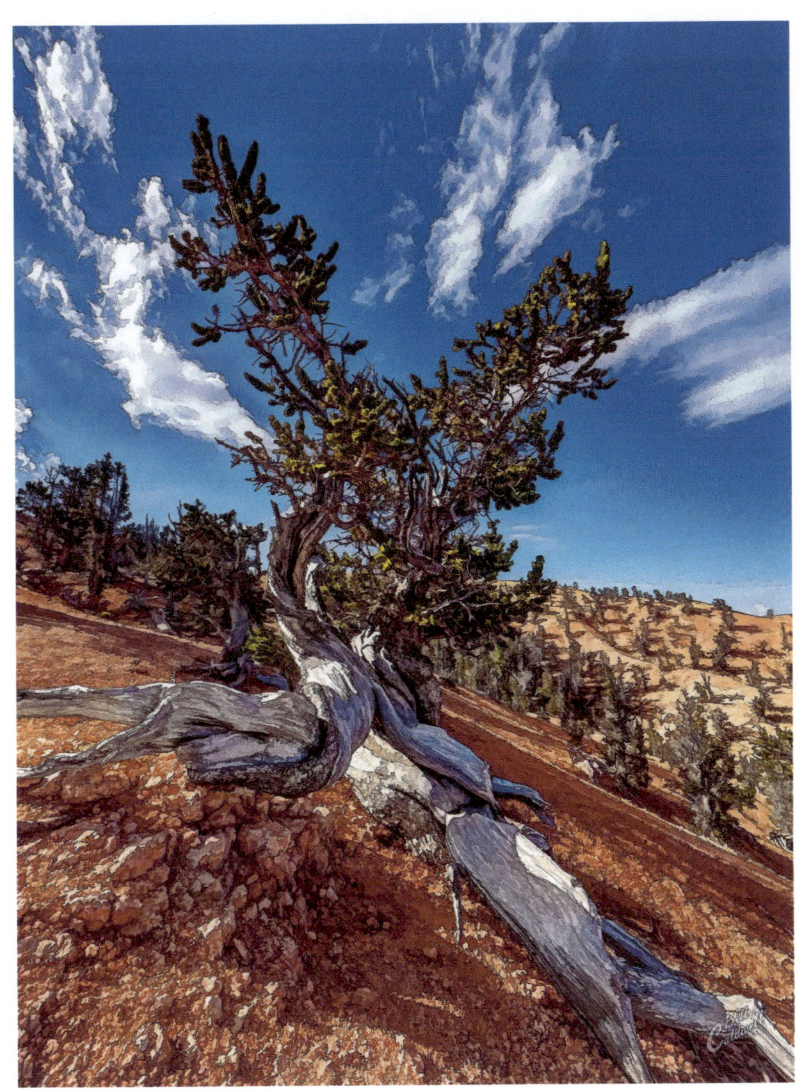

Expanding Wisdom

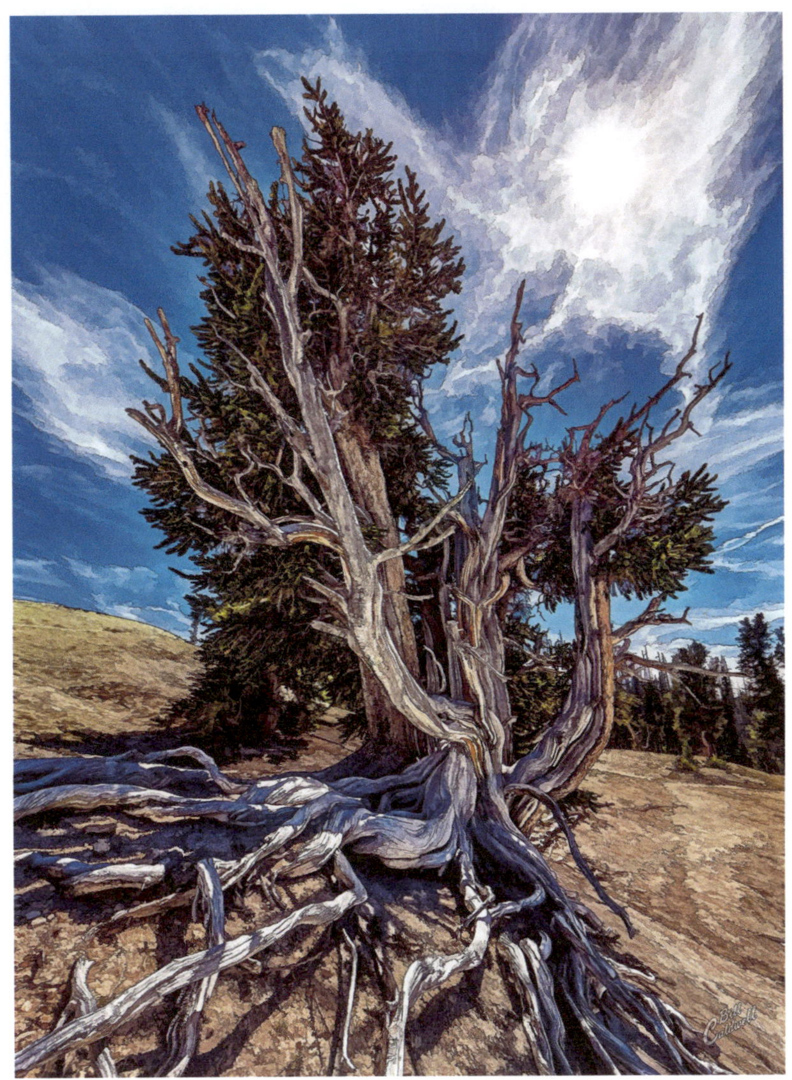

Ancient Expansion

"You practice being the quiet to all the noise, without judgment as to success or failure. Just honor yourself, for the choice to take this time, away from the time that daily owns you. Slowly become the Quiet One."
— Clay Lomakayu

When I was a young man I spent a lot of time surfing. For me, surfing was a spiritual practice, a way to connect with nature and the Universe. Sometimes, when I was sitting on my surfboard just outside the breakers, a group of dolphins would swim by, sometimes jumping and splashing or even surfing the waves themselves. Other times a flock of pelicans would come gliding by just above the water, catching the updraft along the crest of a wave. My feeling of joy, appreciation, and connection with nature was so strong in those moments. Although I haven't surfed for many years now, I still love being near water and especially the movement of water, whether it's the waves of the ocean or a flowing river or just a babbling brook. Water, and especially moving water, has a beautiful energy, a cleansing energy that you can feel in your soul. You can feel that same energy in many places across the globe too, so you don't have to travel very far. And once you connect with that feeling within yourself, you'll never forget it, so you don't necessarily have to be there physically. You can connect with that feeling by looking at a picture of a river, a lake, or a seascape and meditating.

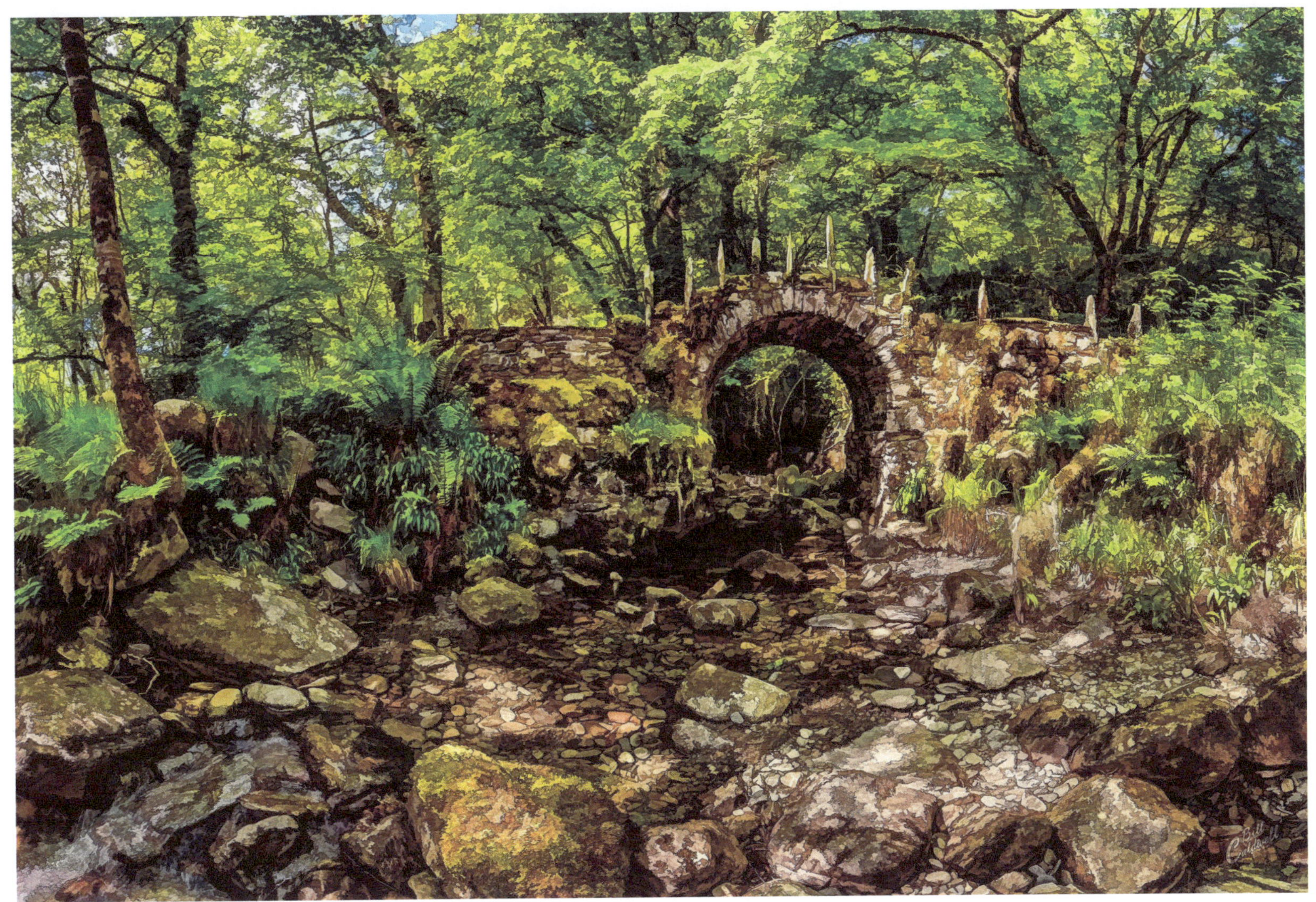

Mystical Bridge

As I sit on a rock listening to the slow movement of water, I begin to see a soft glow forming around the plants, trees, rocks, and water. Nature can be such a calming and joyful lesson at times. Take a walk in the woods, or sit by a stream, and you become one with everything around you. At this place, at this time, at this moment—I am filled with peace.

For me, being in nature, hiking and taking pictures has been an important part of my spiritual practice for a long time now. I can feel a shift in the energy when I'm out in nature or looking up at the stars on a clear night. When I'm hiking in the beauty of nature, there's a feeling of awe and wonder that I have. The Navajo word for beauty also means harmony and balance and it's not just something that you see outside of yourself, it's something that you can feel in your heart. Now when I'm hiking and taking pictures, this is the feeling I have as the outside world of hustle and bustle and human activities disappears. When I'm taking my pictures, I'm in a state of mindful presence, my internal dialogue stops and I'm completely focused on capturing the beauty, spirit, and wonder of that moment.

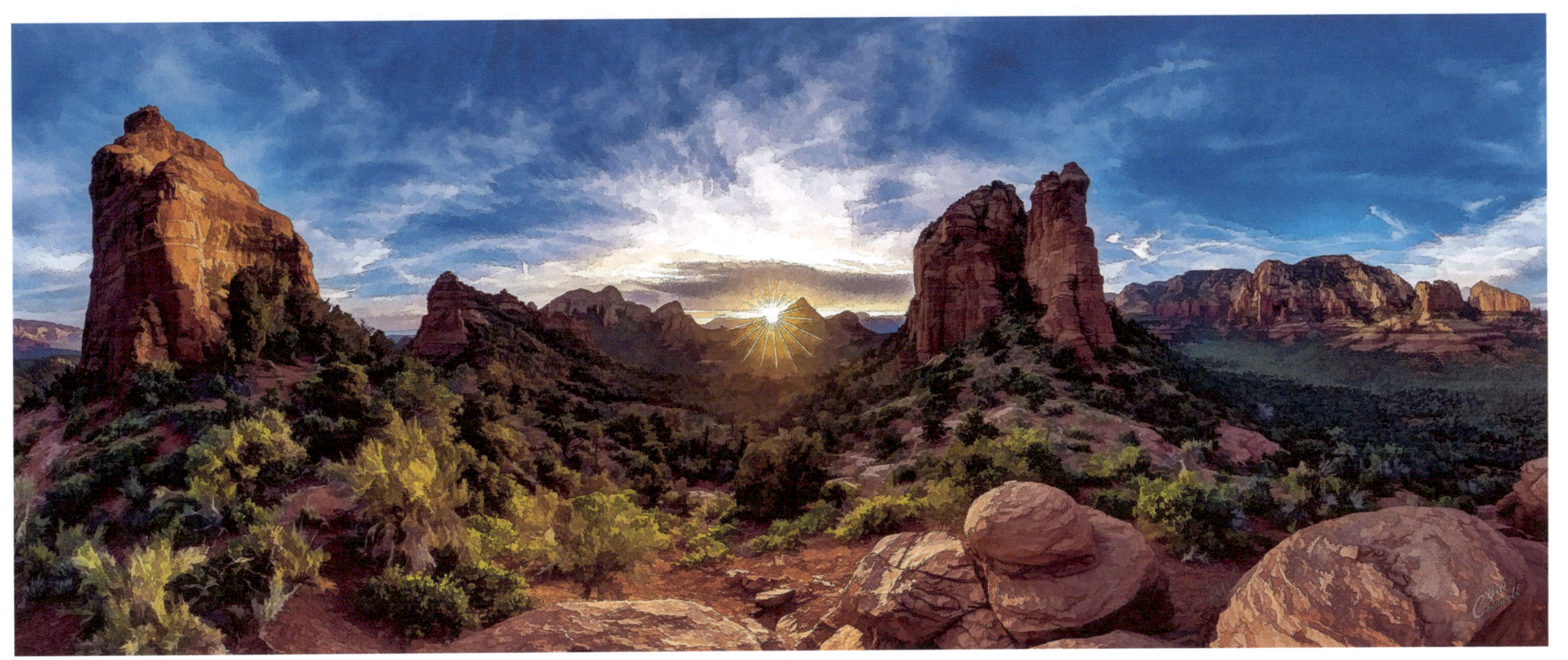

Sacred Beauty

There's an undercurrent of Source Energy flowing just below the surface of everything in the physical universe—a sacred feeling that is beyond the perception of the five physical senses, a sacred beauty that can only be felt when you still your thinking mind and open your heart.

I believe animals are much more important to our spiritual journey than many people would believe—all of the animals, and especially our animal companions. They lift our spirits. They are teachers, healers, companions, and they have the ability to absorb and process negative energy so when their human companions get upset or depressed, they can help alleviate those negative emotions. They also have the ability to take on a portion of our pain and discomfort when we are ill, and to help ease the passing of those who are ready to transition. And sometimes they work together with our spirit guides to help us make decisions or when we are working on important projects. One of the beautiful things about animals is that they live very much in the present moment. They don't obsess about the future or regret the past. And although they have distinct personalities, they have no ego and they are true to themselves.

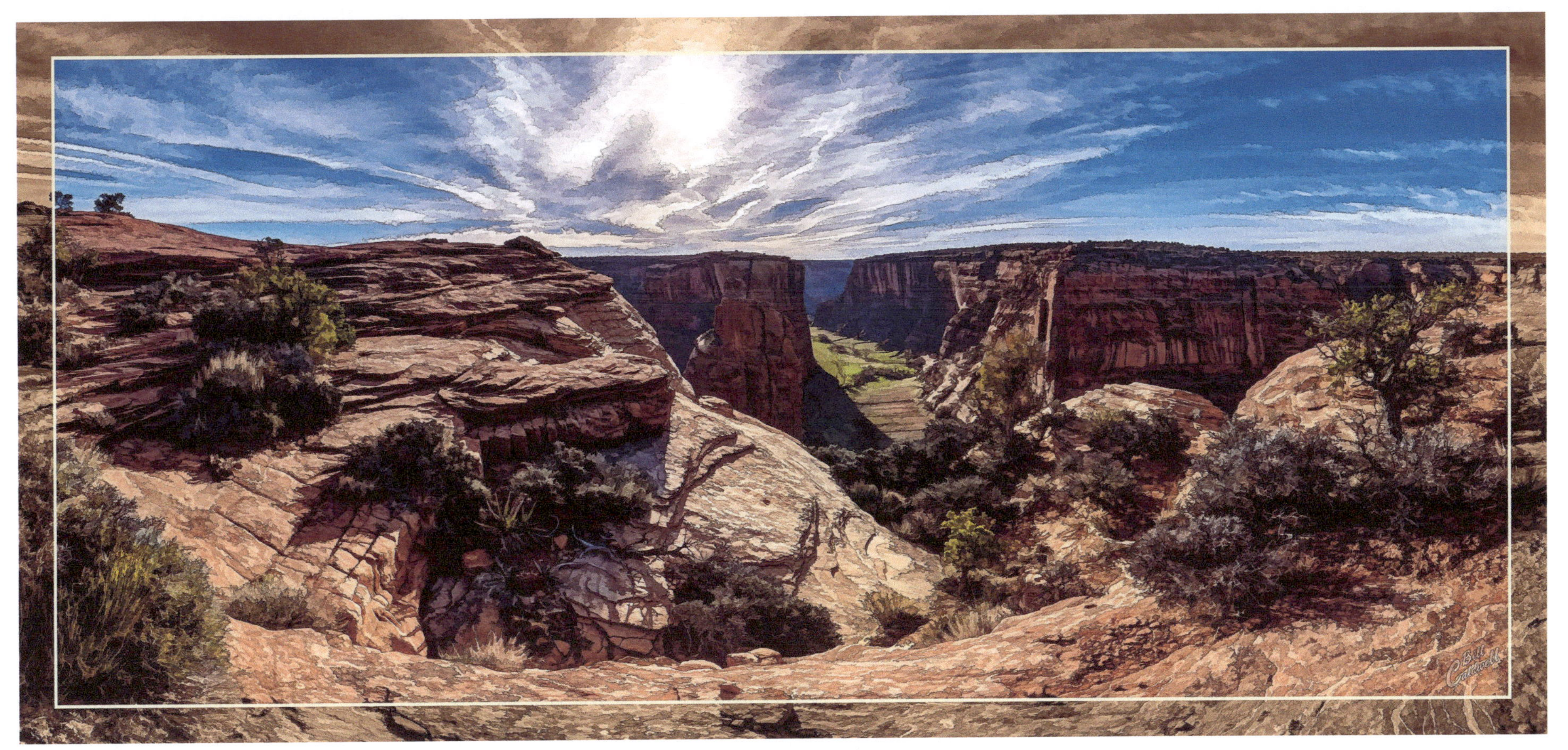

The Corridor

I was visiting Canyon de Chelly and as I was walking towards the canyon, a little blue bird began squawking loudly, over and over again, while flying back and forth between me and the canyon edge. When I got closer to the canyon I noticed he was going to a particular spot near the edge and I was thinking how very insistent he seemed. Then it occurred to me that he was showing me where to take my picture and as soon as I had that thought, he stopped squawking and flew away. This is the spot he was showing me.

> *"I have lived with several Zen masters—all of them cats."*
> — Eckhart Tolle

My wife and I have a friend, Paula Rowe, who is an animal communicator (www.facebook.com/aquariusanimals/). As it turns out, animals are much more aware of what's going on in the world than most people would believe. Their connection with Spirit is unrestricted and they have a lot they would like to tell us. Just like humans, animals are on a spiritual path of growth and expansion and part of that path includes helping us on our path.

Paula connected with our cat Destiny and this is what she had to say. Destiny is part of a group of 13 cats that meet in spirit to talk about their lives, teach each other, and talk about how they can help their humans. Part of a cats mission is to show people how to be strong and graceful. You don't have to do everything other people say. You can have your own mind and be graceful, kind, and respectful; *and* you can say "no." That's a good thing—speak your mind, speak your truth. Sometimes you do things for others, as long as it's not too high a cost for yourself. Cats are good at saying no and that's part of their mission: to teach people how to say no gracefully. Another part of their mission is to teach people balance: stretch, relax, play, nap, and work—balance your time. There's no need to rush through your life. Cats are good at this.

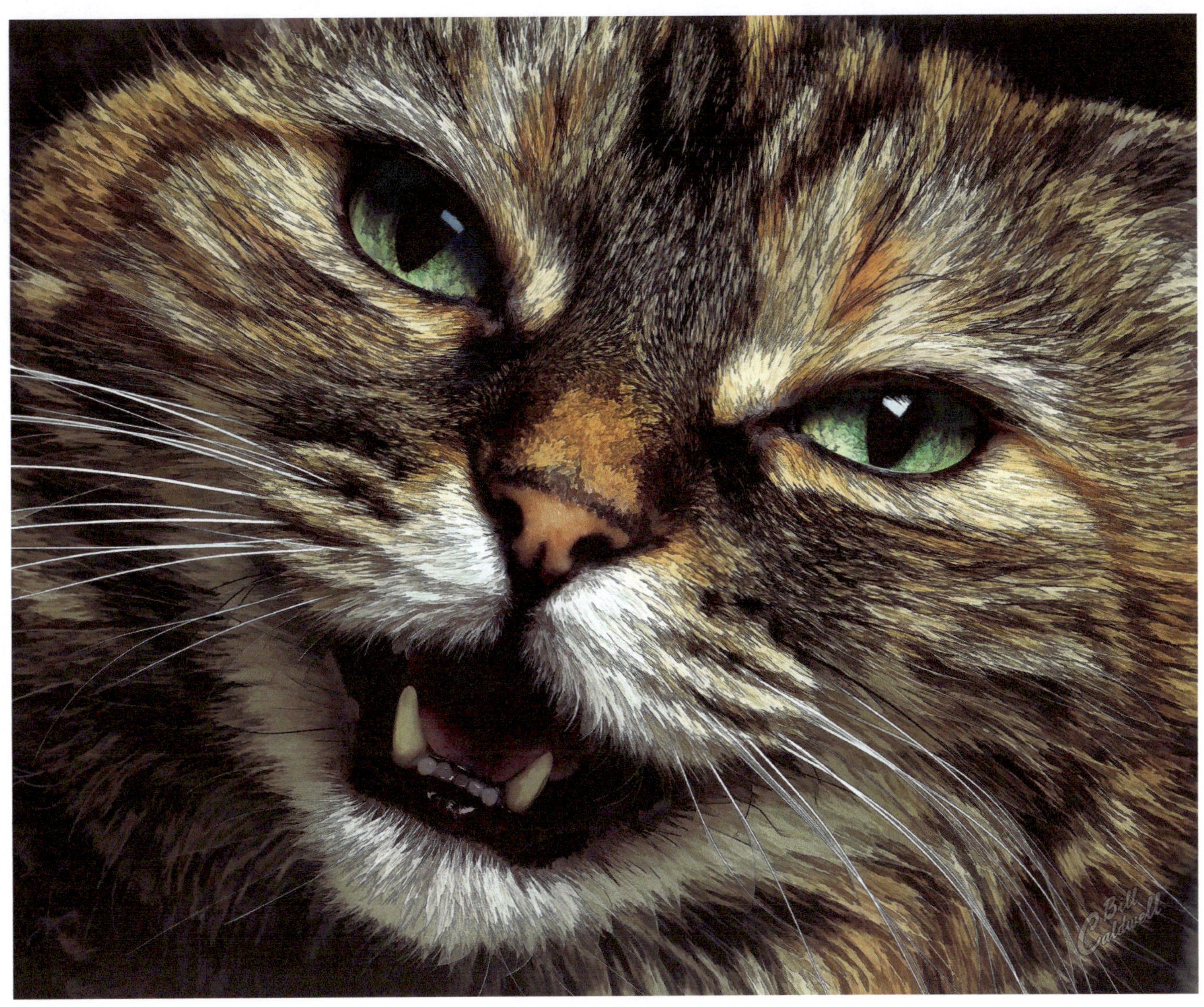

Destiny Speaks

"We wish people would see the true spiritual nature of pets, of all animals, and of each other."

Although I've always had a great love and appreciation for animals, I never understood the full extent of their abilities and purpose until recently. Our friend Paula connected with a horny toad lizard that we met while hiking on a trail near Sedona and and this is what he had to say: "The world is ready to hear our message, not all people are ready but many are, so please put our message out there. A lot of people are at a crossroad—are they going to focus more on the material world or more on the spiritual? People need to work on their connection to Source, learn to listen to their intuition. Just go with the flow, like a river down the mountain. Don't worry about what others are saying or doing, just listen to your intuition, get in your boat and go with the flow. And the more you go with the flow, the more tuned-in you get and the more connected to Source you get. The more you follow your bliss, the higher your vibration will be and the better your life will get. The things you don't like will fall away and the things you like will be in more abundance. Don't worry about what might happen, just go with the flow and be in the now. Focus on the present moment and focus on the good things. Just do it—it's all good!"

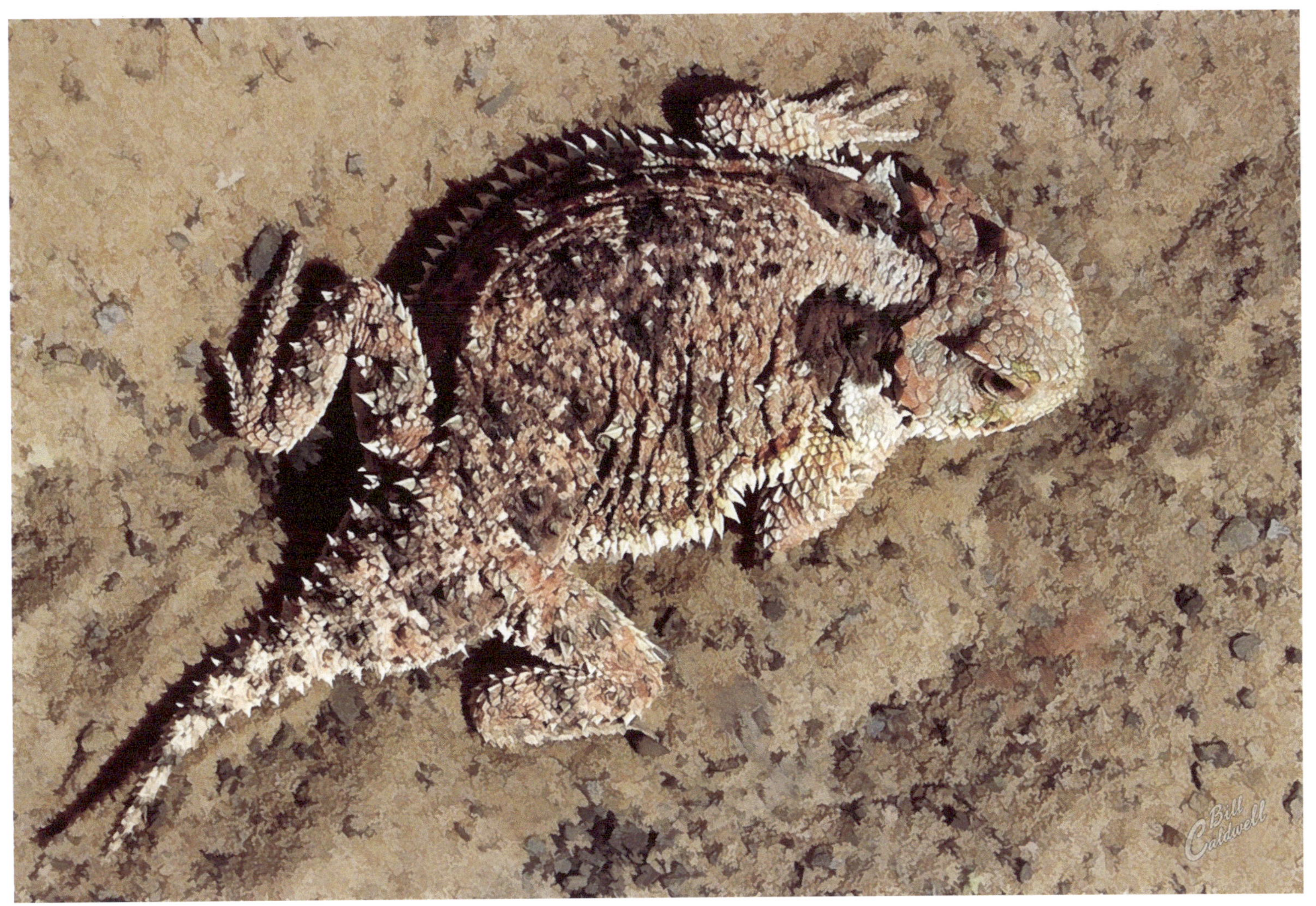

Get Connected

"Get connected, tune-in to Source, trust your intuition, and go with the flow. Just do it—it's all good!"

You're Never Alone

Although it may not seem that way at times, *we are never alone*. We are all connected metaphysically through an unseen network of energy. We all come into this world connected with Source Energy, our spirit guides, teachers, and our higher self (the greater part of Who-You-Really-Are). Sometimes guides and teachers come in the form of spirit animals or totems, but they are all here for the same purpose: to help guide us, teach us, steer us towards our life's purpose, and sometimes to protect us. Although we may not be aware of it, different spirit guides will come into our lives at different times to help us with specific things, while others may stay with us for our entire lives, or many of our lifetimes. As we move forward in our spiritual growth and expansion, new spirit guides will come into our lives to teach us new things and help us move forward on our path. And the guidance we receive comes in many forms: feelings, intuition, curiosities, and very quiet passing thoughts. Sometimes guidance comes in the form of messages from people you meet, TV shows, movies, books, videos, the internet, etc. Such as the time a barber told me about a book she read and later on I kept seeing that book mentioned on the internet until I finally got it and read it.

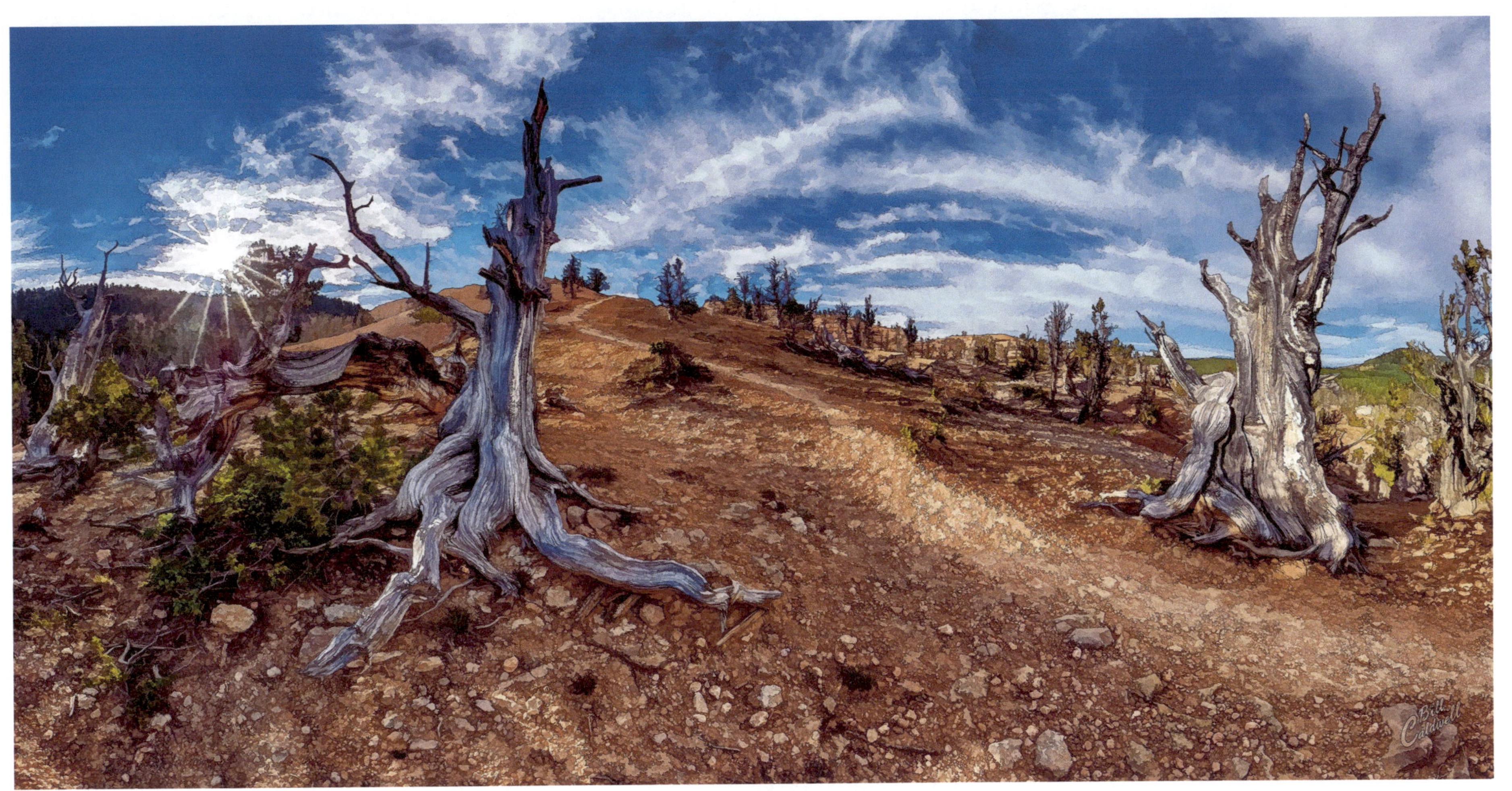

Ancient Knowledge

"You are constantly receiving guidance and assistance from your guides and teachers, and from the universe itself. When you choose consciously to move toward the energy of your soul, you invite that guidance. When you ask the universe to bless you in your effort to align yourself with your soul, you open a passageway between yourself and your guides and teachers." — Gary Zukav

Our heart-felt feelings, and what we call intuition, are actually our spirit guides and higher self talking to us. For example, when you're making a decision, or contemplating doing something, and you have that sinking feeling in the pit of your stomach, then you know your guides are trying to steer you away from that. But when you feel joy, or you just feel relief, then you know that's the direction your guides and higher self are steering you toward. When I was getting close to graduation from college, I applied for a job at a large museum and was accepted, but I had a bad feeling about it. The job wasn't going to start for several months so I had plenty of time to think about it. It would have been a very steady job, a safe job, but every time I thought about it I got this sick, sinking feeling in the pit of my stomach. I ended up declining the job offer. I now know my spirit guides were steering me away from that job, not because it was a bad job, but because it was not a "path with a heart." It would not have served my spiritual growth at that time.

Although I can't see my spirit guides, I know they are around. Someone that I've known for a long time, and trust, can see spirit beings and has told me about some of mine. Sometimes when I meditate I can see them and I can feel their love. I've had associations with big cats in many lifetimes and I have several spirit guides that take the form of big cats. One of them takes the form of a black jaguar and another takes the form of a golden lioness. Sometimes I can sense their presence and sometimes when I'm hiking, if I start tripping for no apparent reason, I know the lioness is playing with me! These two have been with me for many lifetimes and have protected me from danger more than once in this physical lifetime. Know that at all times, our spirit guides and teachers are acting out of love. They have great love for us and they want what's best for our spiritual growth and the expansion of our consciousness. Each step we take in our spiritual journey is eagerly anticipated and met with great joy and appreciation. As Abraham-Hicks often says, "There is great love here for you."

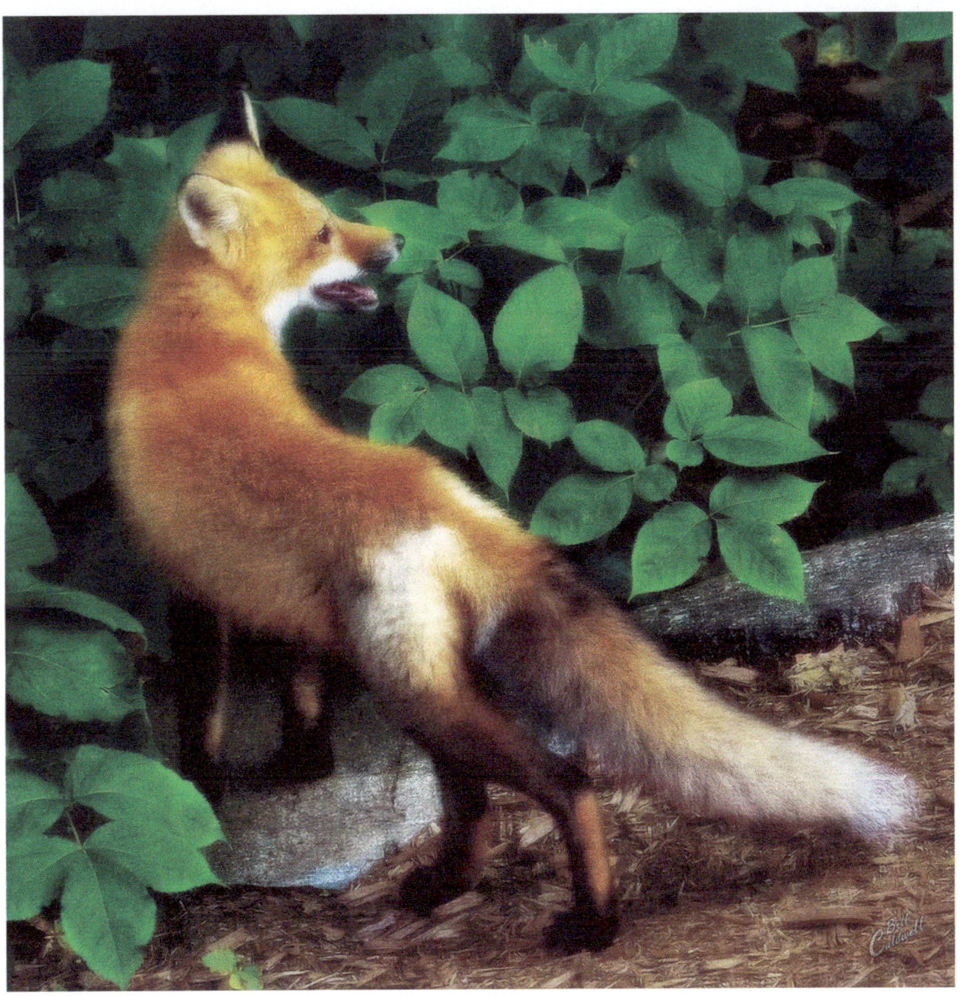

Bella

Each step we take in our spiritual journey is eagerly anticipated and met with great joy and appreciation.

Sometimes when I'm hiking, I feel like I'm being guided to certain places at certain times to take certain pictures. As a landscape photographer, I love having beautiful, dramatic clouds in my landscape pictures so I'm always on the lookout for a beautiful sky. I'm also thinking about when the best time of day would be for the best lighting. The interesting thing is that I sometimes end up at places and times that I wasn't mentally planning on, and those pictures turn out to be some of my favorites. Like when I took the picture on the next page, "Doe Mountain Magic." I climbed up the mesa before dawn thinking that I would get a nice sunrise picture at a particular spot that I had been to before. As it turns out, the sunrise picture was not what I envisioned, but after I finished taking that picture, I started wandering around looking for other spots along the edge of the mesa. I didn't have a particular spot in mind, I just felt like going towards the other side of the mesa. By the time I arrived at the place in this picture, some dramatic clouds had moved in and I knew this was going to be a beautiful picture. Although I didn't get the picture I was planning on, I believe I got the picture I was supposed to get! I realize now that I must have been guided by something outside of my logical thinking mind—my spirit guides and my higher self. I took that picture a few years ago and since that time I've been practicing tuning in more frequently and more consciously to that guidance. In my experience, this type of guidance is very subtle and easily drowned out by my logical mind and whatever is going on around me. So I have to practice listening and tuning in more consciously so I can recognize this guidance.

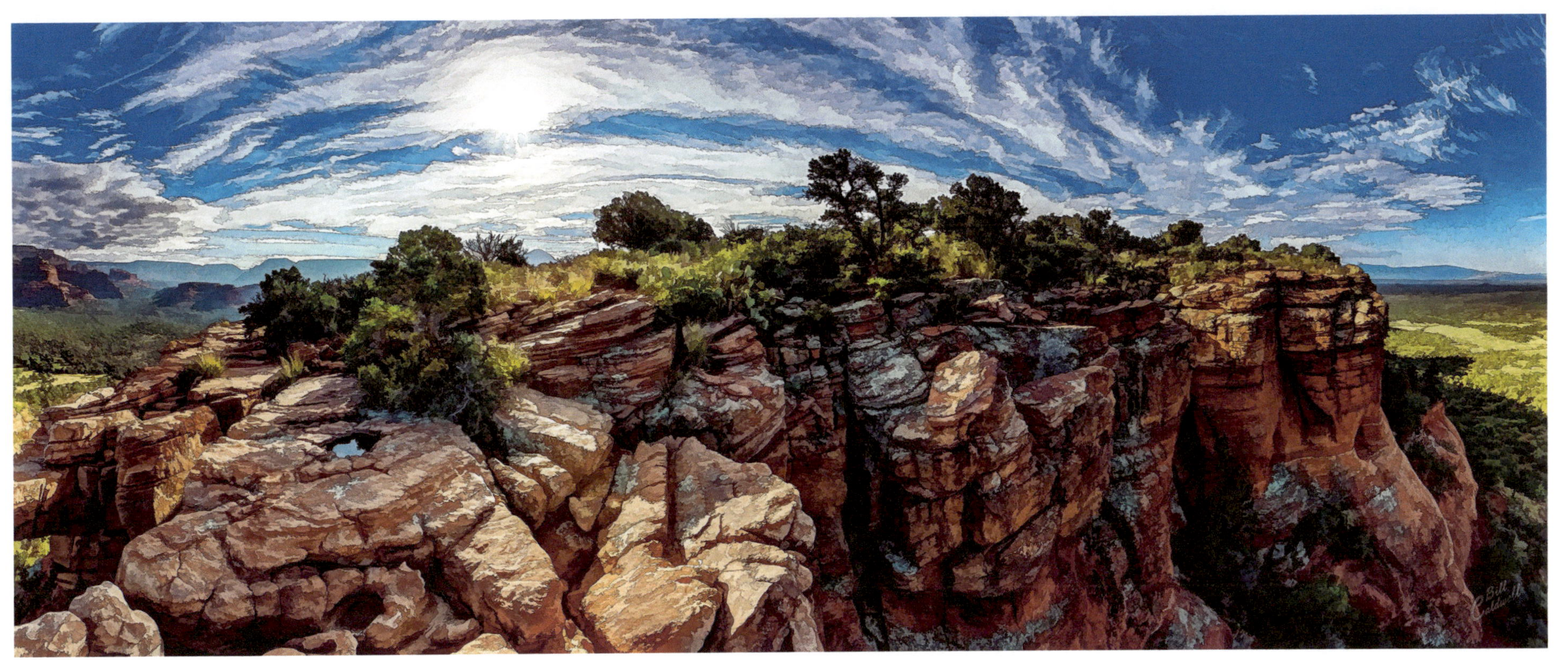

Doe Mountain Magic

Know that you're always receiving guidance, even if you don't realize it.
Know that at any given time, you're right where you need to be at that moment.

Transforming, Transcending, & Perspective

If you look at the history of human thought and science, you'll see that our human perspective has changed dramatically over the centuries. There was a time when people believed the Earth was flat and that it was the center of the universe and the stars merely a thin shell of lights surrounding us. We now know that the Earth is just one of several planets orbiting around our Sun which, in turn, is just one of many billions of stars orbiting around the center of our Milky Way galaxy. And with the help of the Hubble Space Telescope, we now know that our Milky Way galaxy is just one of many billions of galaxies. Talk about a change in perspective! But it doesn't stop there—we are still changing and evolving. Neale Donald Walsch and Gary Zukav talk about a higher perspective, the perspective of the soul. Many things that don't make sense to us from our physical human perspective, make perfect sense when seen from the perspective of our higher self or soul. As individuals, and humankind in general, we are evolving and expanding our knowledge, awareness, and consciousness. This broadens our perspective, which changes our perception—and this in turn, changes our experience of the world.

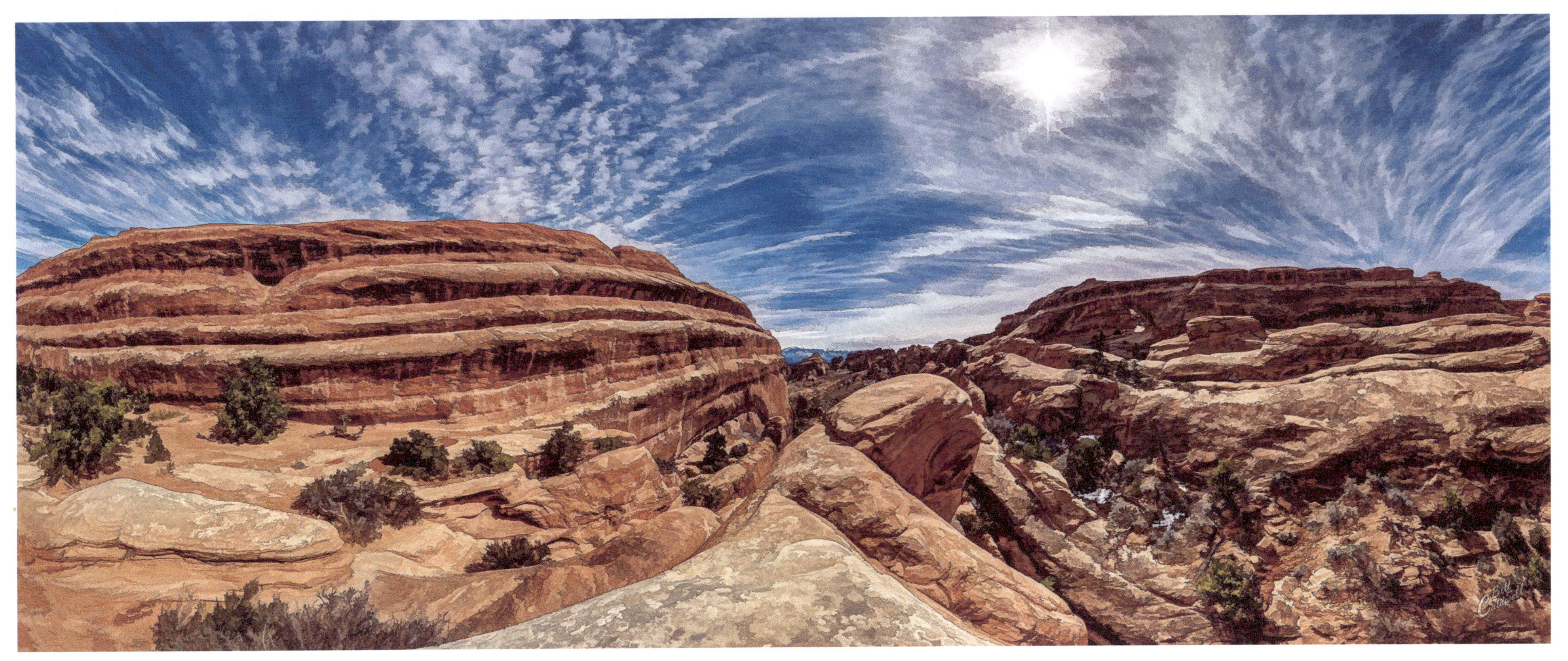

Folds in Time

"Fifteen hundred years ago, everybody 'knew' that the Earth was the center of the universe. Five hundred years ago, everybody 'knew' that the Earth was flat. And 15 minutes ago, you 'knew' that humans were alone on this planet. Imagine what you'll 'know' tomorrow." — Agent K "Men in Black"

I studied astronomy in high school and college and this dramatically changed my perspective. All of the celestial bodies; the planets, the solar system, the stars, nebulae, black holes, quasars, and galaxies—all of these things were fascinating and beautiful to me. It quickly became apparent to me that the sheer size and scale of the physical universe is incredible, beyond comprehension. And although our scientists have learned quite a lot during the last few hundred years, it's also apparent there's so much more we don't know, even right here on our own planet. Until recently, biologists believed that all life on earth was dependent upon photosynthesis—plants and phytoplankton being the basis of all food chains on the planet. Then oceanographers discovered living ecosystems around hot geothermal vents deep in the ocean that used chemosynthesis instead of photosynthesis. This was something that had never been seen before. So we are constantly learning new things, constantly expanding our understanding and awareness.

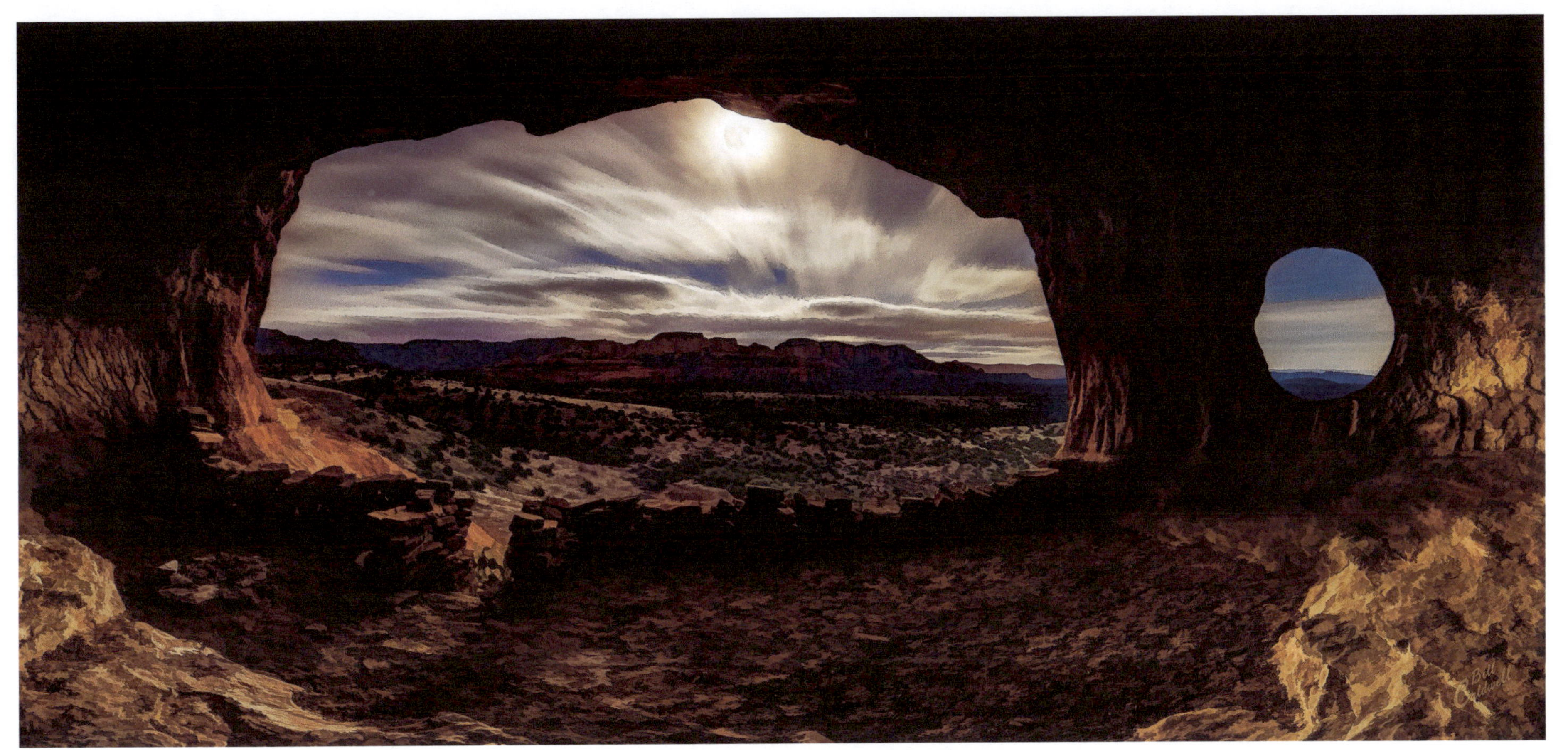

Shaman's Cave by Moonlight

*We are evolving and expanding our knowledge, awareness, and consciousness.
This broadens our perspective, which changes our perception—and this in turn,
changes our experience of the world.*

When I was in high school I started reading a series of books by Carlos Castaneda. In these books, Carlos writes about his experiences with don Juan Matus, a Yaqui Indian and shaman from Sonora Mexico. In one of these experiences don Juan talks about "a path with a heart." This quotation struck a powerful cord in me and ever since then I've tried to live my life by following "a path with a heart." We are all on a spiritual journey of learning, growth, and expansion, whether we're conscious of it or not. There are many paths we can take and we all have our own pathway. There is no right or wrong path—there is only the path that you choose. So why not choose the path that resonates with your heart and soul?

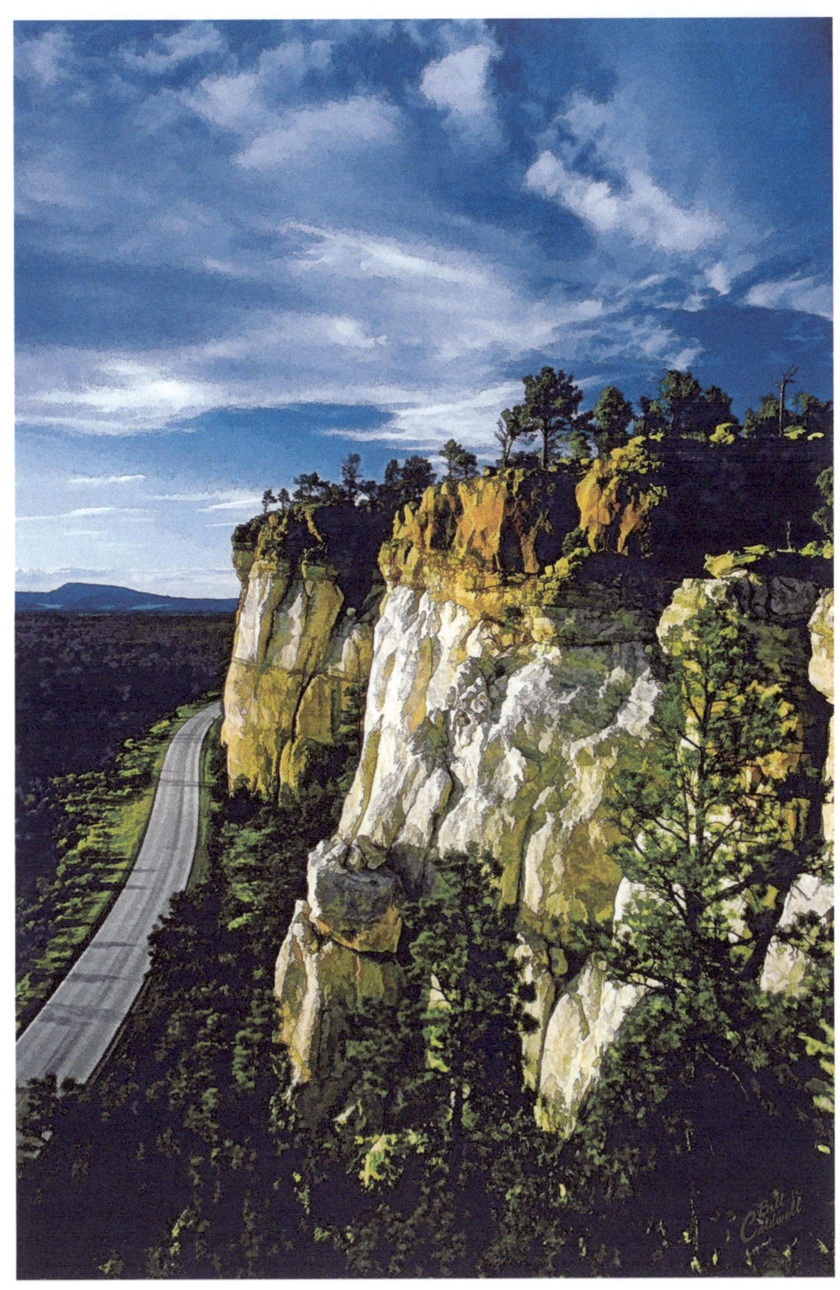

The Road Less Traveled

"...Two roads diverged in a wood, and I—I took the one less traveled by, and that has made all the difference." — Robert Frost

I've been curious about science, metaphysics, and spiritual subjects since I was a teenager so I started reading books about these subjects. Although I wasn't consciously pursuing a spiritual path then, I did learn about the principle of taking responsibility for our own decisions and actions. This idea resonated with me and I took it to heart. I know now that making responsible choices is an important part of living life consciously. About 10 years ago, after reading certain books and going to certain spiritual seminars, both my wife and I realized that one of the primary reasons we are here in the physical world is for the purpose of spiritual growth and expansion. At that point we both began following our spiritual paths in a more deliberate, conscious manner. Neither one of us subscribe to any of the organized religions—that just never resonated with either one of us. We seek spiritual truth and knowledge wherever we may find it, whether it's in a church, at school, at seminars, on the internet, TV, the movies, through meditation, or reading books and articles.

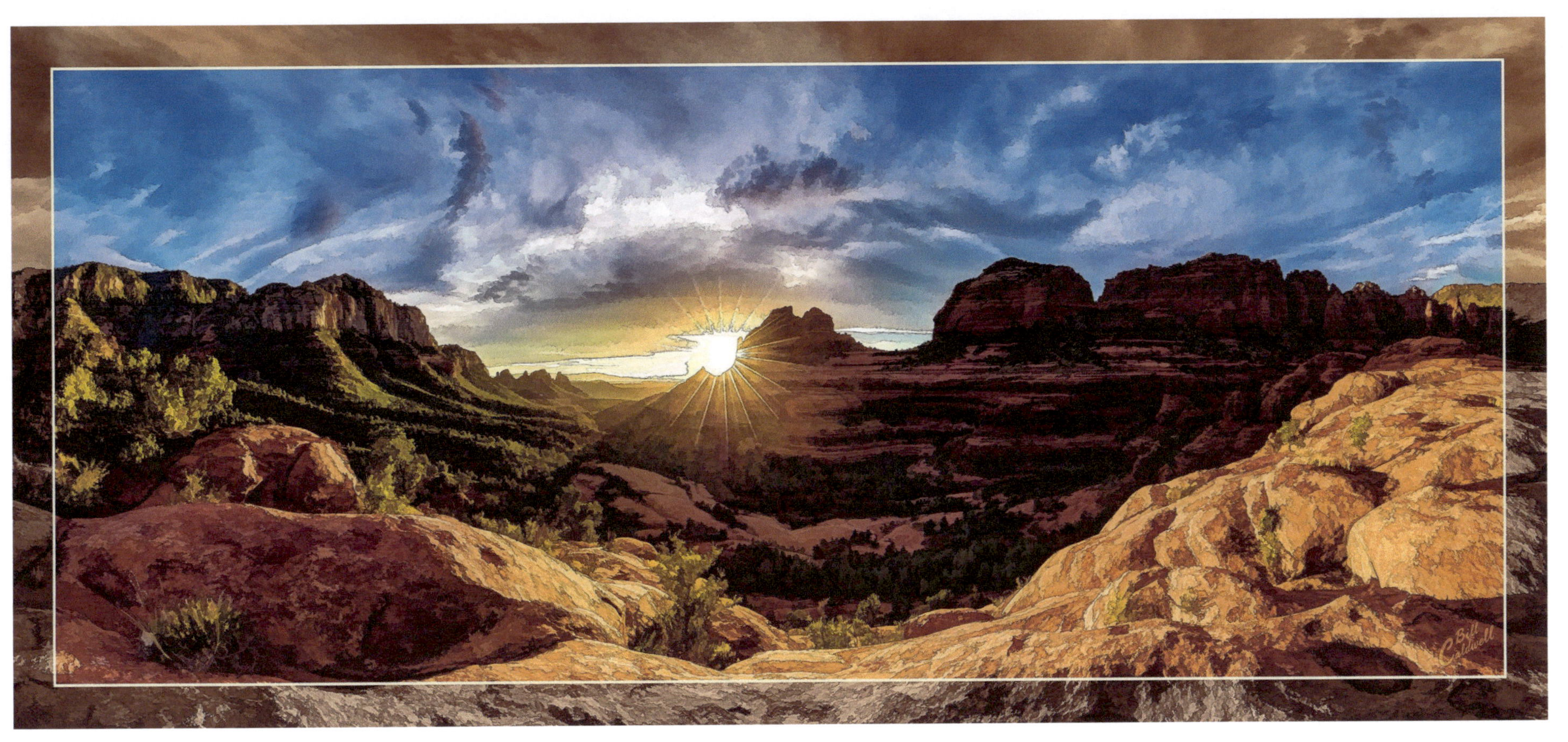

Red Rock Spirit

"The decisions that you make and the actions that you take upon the Earth are the means by which you evolve. At each moment you choose the intentions that will shape your experiences and those things upon which you will focus your attention. These choices affect your evolutionary process. This is so for each person. If you choose unconsciously, you evolve unconsciously. If you choose consciously, you evolve consciously." — Gary Zukav

Reading books, meditating, going to seminars, or listening to spiritual teachers online are all good ways to keep moving forward on our spiritual path—but not just any book, seminar, or teacher—pick the ones that spark your natural curiosity and resonate with you. We are always transforming; learning, growing, and expanding our awareness. Especially now, we are all going through a major transformation, as individuals and the human race as a whole. We are transforming from five-sensory humans to what Gary Zukav calls multi-sensory humans. We are learning new ways of looking at the world, new ways of thinking about the world. We are tuning in to our sixth sense and opening up our connection with our nonphysical guides, teachers, and our connection with Universal Consciousness. Every individual takes part in this whether they're conscious of it or not because we are all connected metaphysically with each other, with our higher selves, with the Universe. The more you learn about yourself, about Who-You-Really-Are and the gifts you have to share, the more you benefit and the more the *whole Universe benefits*. The whole Universe is living through you and through every being and the more you grow and expand, the more the whole Universe grows and expands!

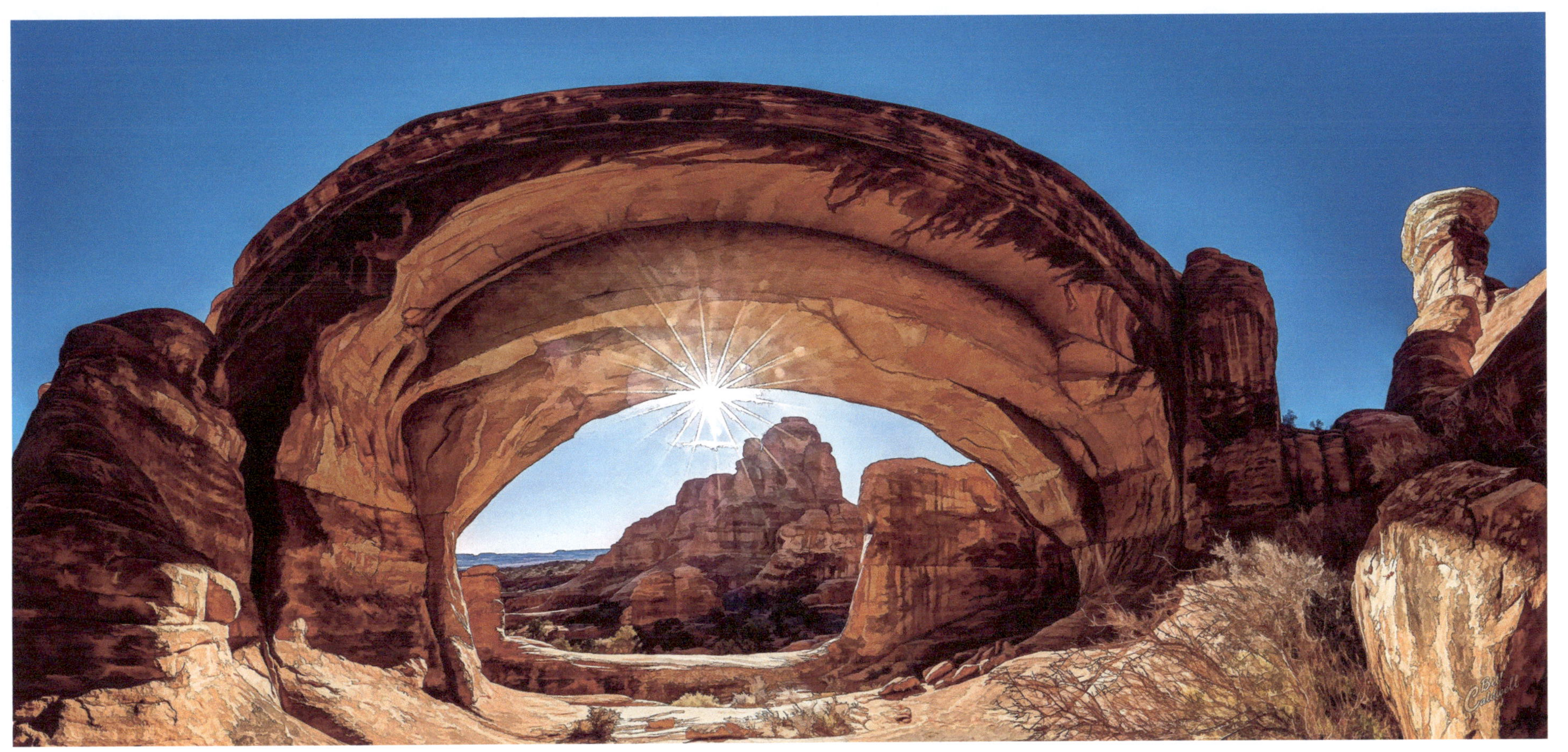

The Ancient Doorway

"When you're in the way of waking up, and finding out who you really are, what you do is what the whole universe is doing at the place that you call here and now. You are something the whole universe is doing in the same way that a wave is something that the ocean is doing. The real you is not a puppet which life pushes around, the real deep down you is the whole Universe." — Alan Watts

The thing we need to pay attention to as we explore new ideas, philosophies, and belief systems is the feeling that goes along with them and the energy of those new concepts. Does it feel good to *you*, does it resonate with *you*, does it make sense to *you*? Of course, this also applies to any decision we have to make in life. We need to stay tuned in to our intuition and heart-felt feelings. Nobody but *you* should decide what you choose to embrace and believe in. When you read a new book or listen to a spiritual teacher and you feel the joy of new learning and new understanding, and it resonates with you, then you know you are in alignment with your higher self. If you read something or hear something that gives you a bad feeling or it simply does not resonate with you, then you know that's not the direction you want to go. When you read something or hear something, pay attention to the way you feel. Listen to your heart. I was watching a TV program called The Voice (a singing competition) and one of the contestants, a young lady, was talking about taking singing lessons as a young girl, and she said, "When I felt the joy, I knew this is what I wanted to do with my life." Do you feel the joy?

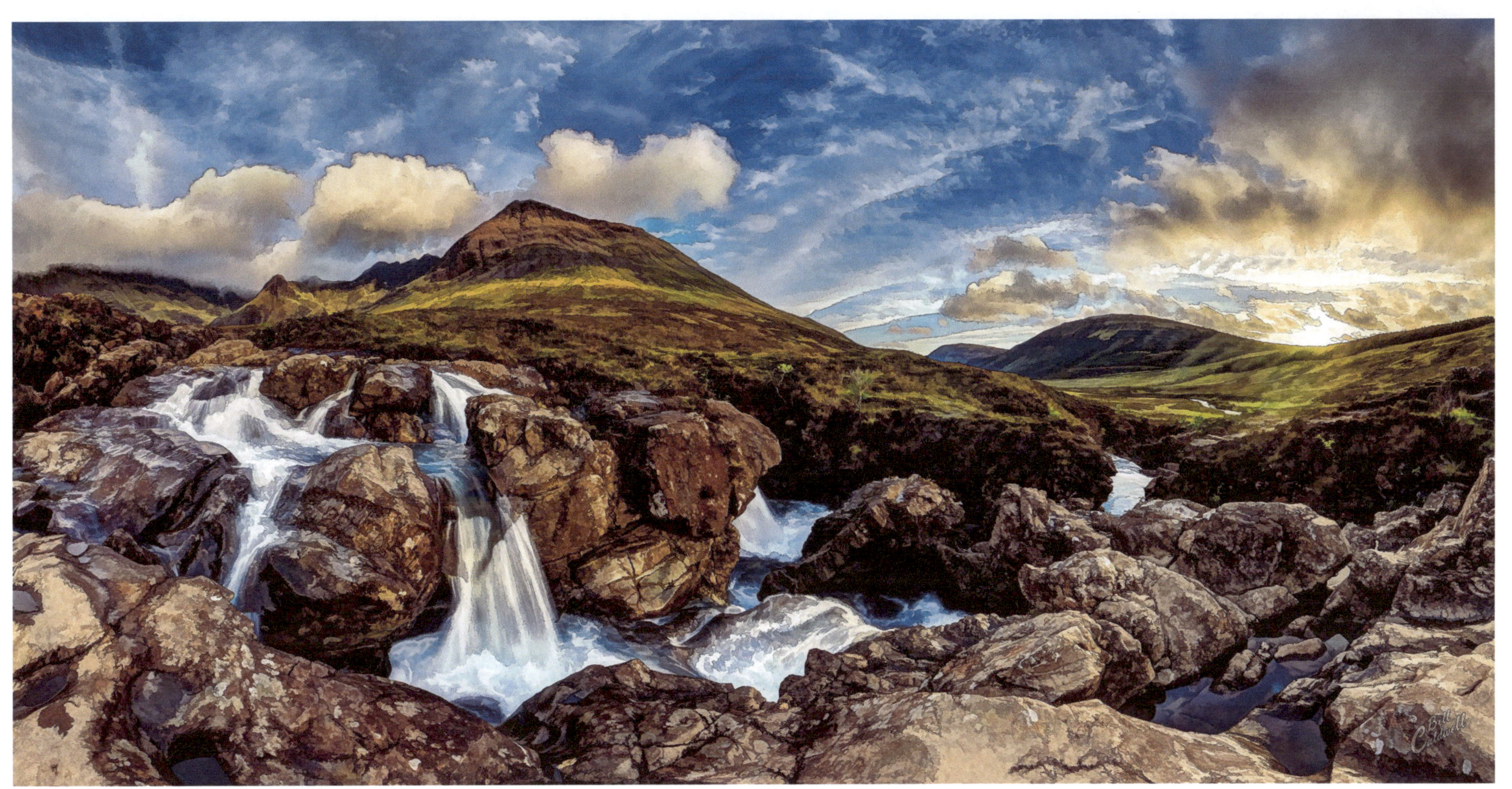

Follow Your Joy

"Let yourself be silently drawn by the stronger pull of what you really love.
When you do things from your soul, you feel a river moving in you, a joy."
— Rumi

I believe that an important part of our spiritual growth and expansion is fostering an attitude of open-mindedness and being open to the idea that there's more to the world than meets the eye, more than what science or religion can show us. The spiritual path we take and the decisions we make may or may not be the same as those of the people around us—even if those people are our family members, relatives, or best friends. Just because our friends and family subscribe to a particular religion, spiritual practice, or philosophy, doesn't mean that we have to do the same. Following our own path may, at times, take courage—the courage to go against the grain of the people around us. If we're going to follow a deliberate spiritual path then we have to be willing to look at alternatives; alternative ways of thinking about spirituality and the universe. We need to be willing to explore different philosophies and beliefs. Discussing different beliefs and philosophies with other people is one thing, but when somebody tries to sell you on their beliefs, tries to convince you their belief is right and yours is wrong, then you have to wonder about their motives. What is their agenda? Your feelings and beliefs are just as valid as anyone else's. Sometimes we simply have to go with our "gut" and ignore what other people are telling us.

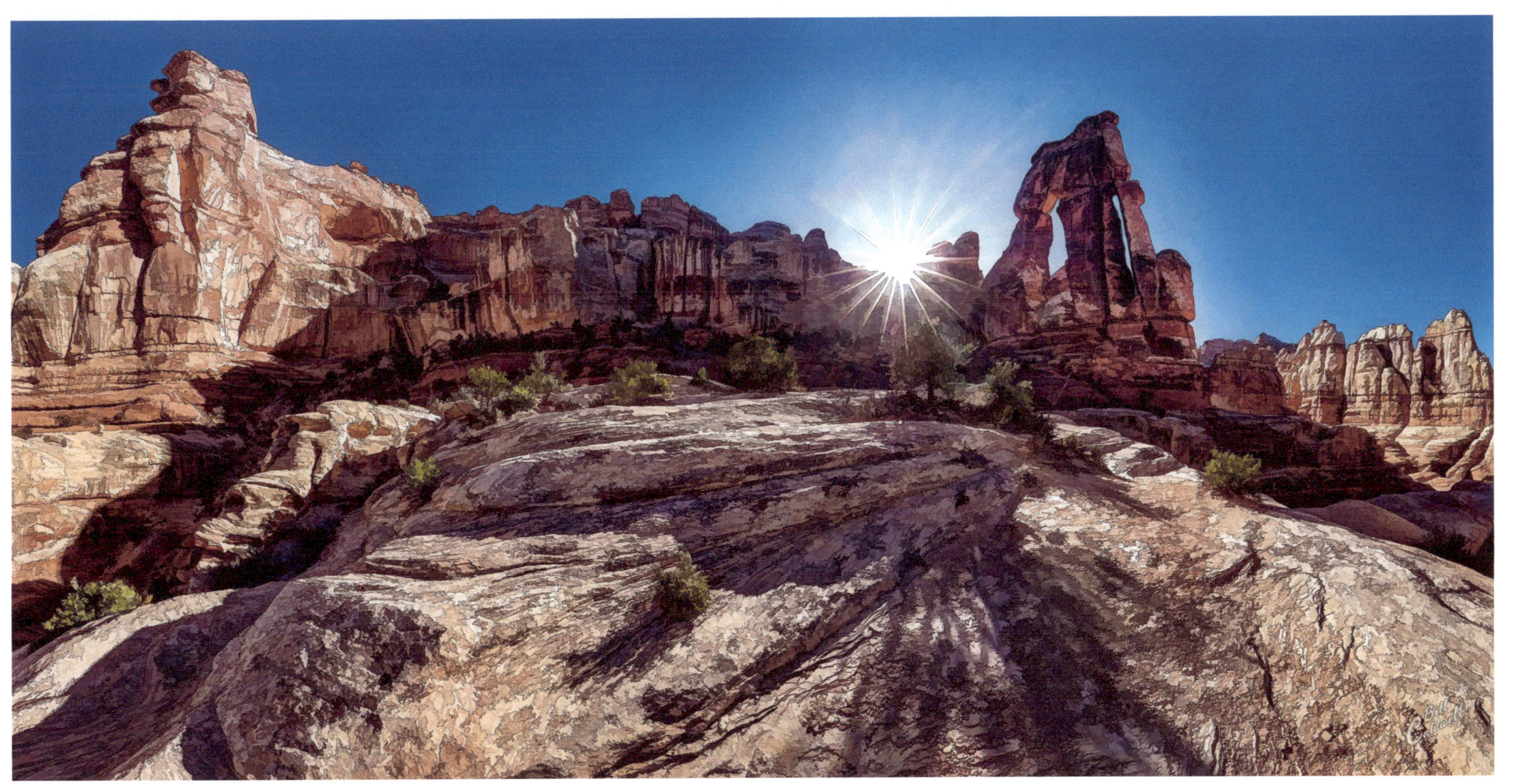

Druid Arch Sanctum

"You do an experiment because your own philosophy makes you want to know the result. It's too hard, and life is too short, to spend your time doing something because someone else has said it's important. You must feel the thing yourself..." — Isidor I. Rabi

Neale Donald Walsch recommends asking ourselves two questions when contemplating any action or decision: "Is this who I am?" and "Is this who I want to be?" I think this is very good advice. You need to develop a sense of what's *right for you* at any given time in spite of what others might be telling you. This applies to both our spiritual beliefs and the decisions that we make every day. This is part of finding our own path through life. And there's no need for you to try and convince anyone else that you're right, because spiritual beliefs can't be proved or disproved. Don't be concerned about what other people are doing or saying, good or bad—or what you judge to be good or bad. Simply do what you feel is right for you and let others be as they are, there's no need for judgement. We are all on journeys of learning, growth, and expansion and there's no right or wrong path.

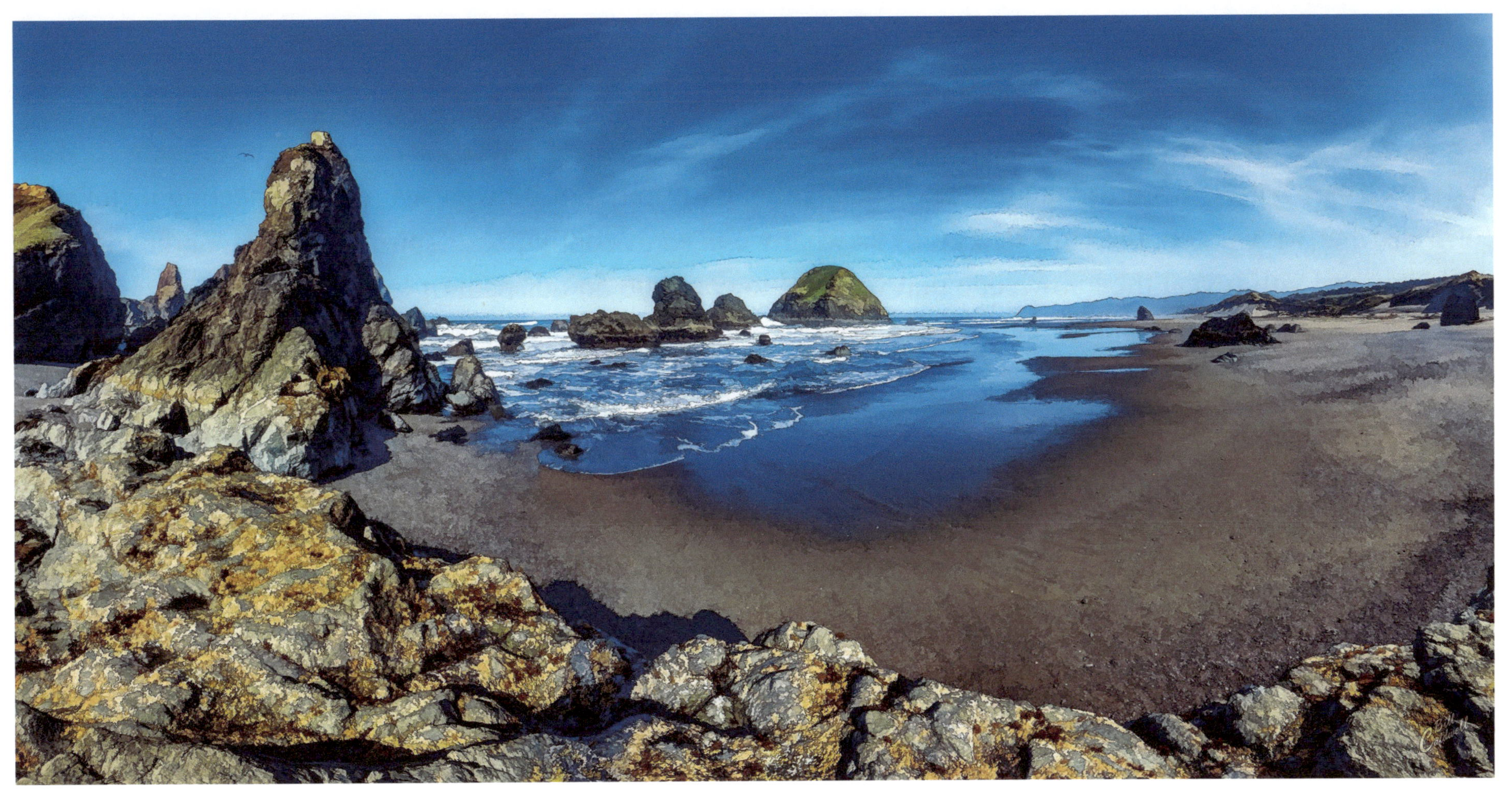

Stand in Your Truth

*Stand strong in your beliefs. Don't worry about what other people are saying
or doing or believing. Trust your own intuition and listen to your heart.
Listen to what resonates with your heart and soul. Stand strong in your truth.*

As we live our lives, the Universe sees what we're doing, sees our efforts, sees that we're moving forward and gives us what we need to take the next step. Although it may not be what we were expecting or take the form of what we wanted, the Universe gives us what we *need* to continue our spiritual growth and expansion. The Universe will reveal the knowledge that we need to continue on our path of learning. Each time we take a step forward, our little world and our concept of the universe expands a bit more and our state of consciousness rises. The Universe sees this and will put in our path things we need to continue our growth. You may notice a particular book at a bookstore or hear about a spiritual seminar and feel attracted or curious about it. We need to stay tuned in to our intuition and feelings and follow our natural curiosity. When I was in high school one of my teachers mentioned Carlos Castaneda's books and I became very curious so I started reading those books, and those books got me curious about other books and ideas. And more recently, when I was getting my hair cut, I was talking to the barber about books we've read and she mentioned "The Four Agreements" by don Miguel Ruiz. It sounded interesting to me but I didn't pick it up for some time. Finally, after I had seen this book mentioned several times on various websites, I bought it and I'm so glad I did.

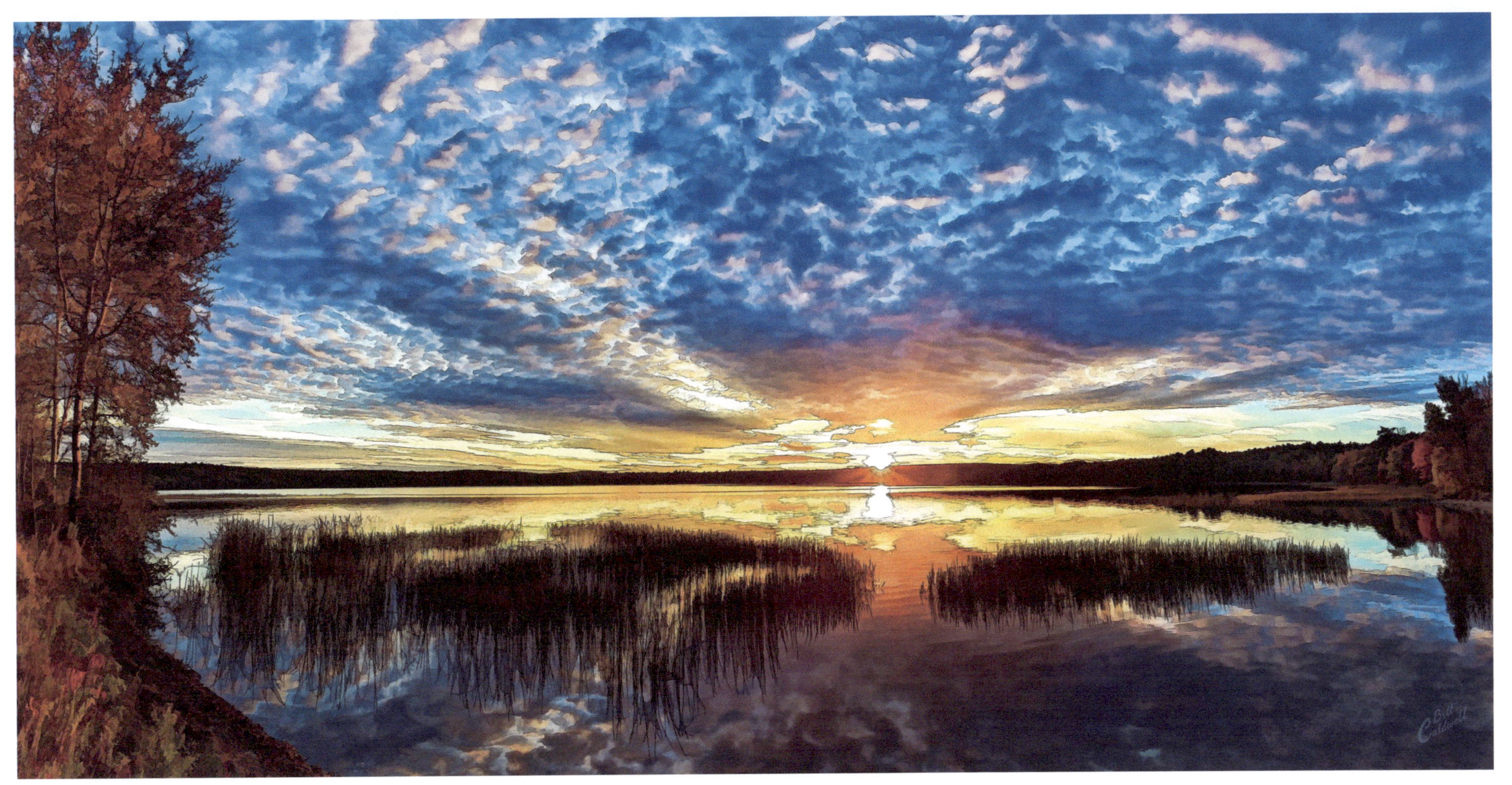

The Universe Listens

"Let your dominant intent be to feel good which means be playful, have fun, laugh often, look for reasons to appreciate and practice the art of appreciation. And as you practice it, the universe, who has been watching you practice, will give you constant opportunities to express it." — Abraham-Hicks

As humans, we have a tendency to follow habitual patterns of thought and behavior, so it's important to keep an open mind and to remain flexible in our thinking. To foster a willingness to explore new philosophies, spiritual ideas, and ways of looking at things. Throughout our lives, the Universe gives us challenges and opportunities to become more. To become more than what we are at this time—more compassionate, more understanding, more gracious. At these times we have a chance to rise above ourselves, but we have to recognize these moments for what they are. This is part of living life consciously.

When I was a young man I thought there was something wrong with gay people, some sort of mental illness. Of course this was a product of my upbringing and the prejudices of the people around me. Although I believed this thought at the time, I never felt comfortable with it. I always had a bad feeling about it. But after reading articles and seeing movies that addressed this issue, combined with some thoughtful contemplation, I came to the realization that gay people were simply being *who they are*—being who they were created to be. One book I read said one of the reasons gays (or anyone who's different than ourselves) are here, is to teach us acceptance and unconditional love. This resonated as the truth to me. If you want to follow a deliberate spiritual path, watch out for habitual patterns of thought and behavior. Don't be afraid to explore other philosophies, spiritual beliefs, and ways of looking at the world. Always listen to your heart, trust your intuition, and trust what resonates with your soul.

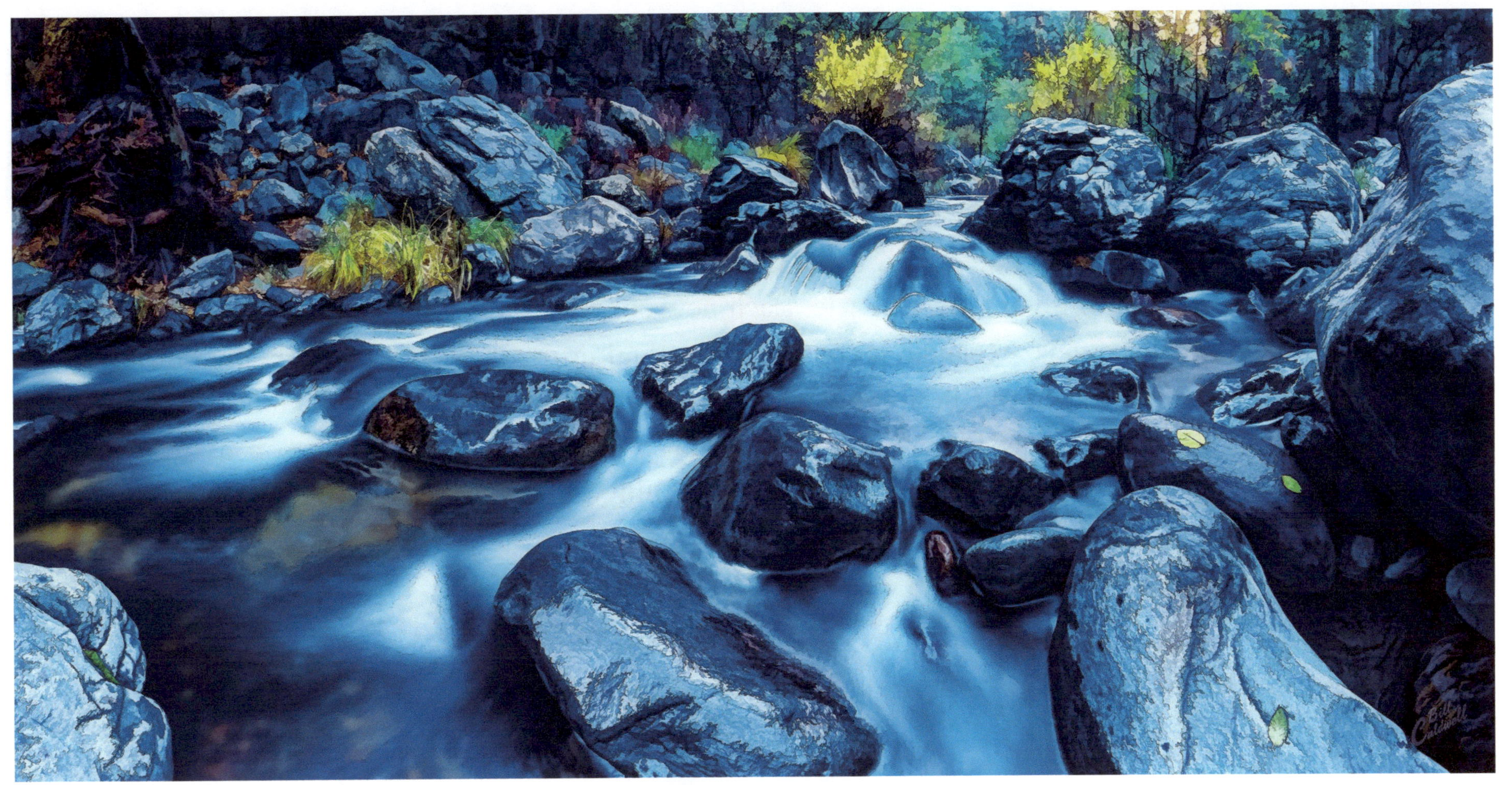

The Challenge

Throughout our lives, the Universe gives us challenges and opportunities to become more. To become more than what we are at this time—more compassionate, more understanding, more gracious. At these times we have a chance to rise above ourselves, but we have to recognize these moments for what they are. This is part of living life consciously.

About 10 years ago I realized that with each new book I read, each new concept I learned, I had to let go of certain older ideas, opinions, attitudes, and beliefs. No single book or spiritual teacher has all the answers. They each contribute pieces of a very large puzzle. Each new concept, philosophy, or belief is just a stepping stone that will widen our horizons, expand our consciousness, and bring us further along on our spiritual path. We don't want to become rigid in our thinking or beliefs—we need to be mentally flexible. Rigid thinking, religious dogma, and rigid belief systems will keep us from growing and expanding, stop us from moving forward; or at the very least, slow us down. We have to be willing to let go of old ideas, beliefs, and attitudes that no longer serve our higher good.

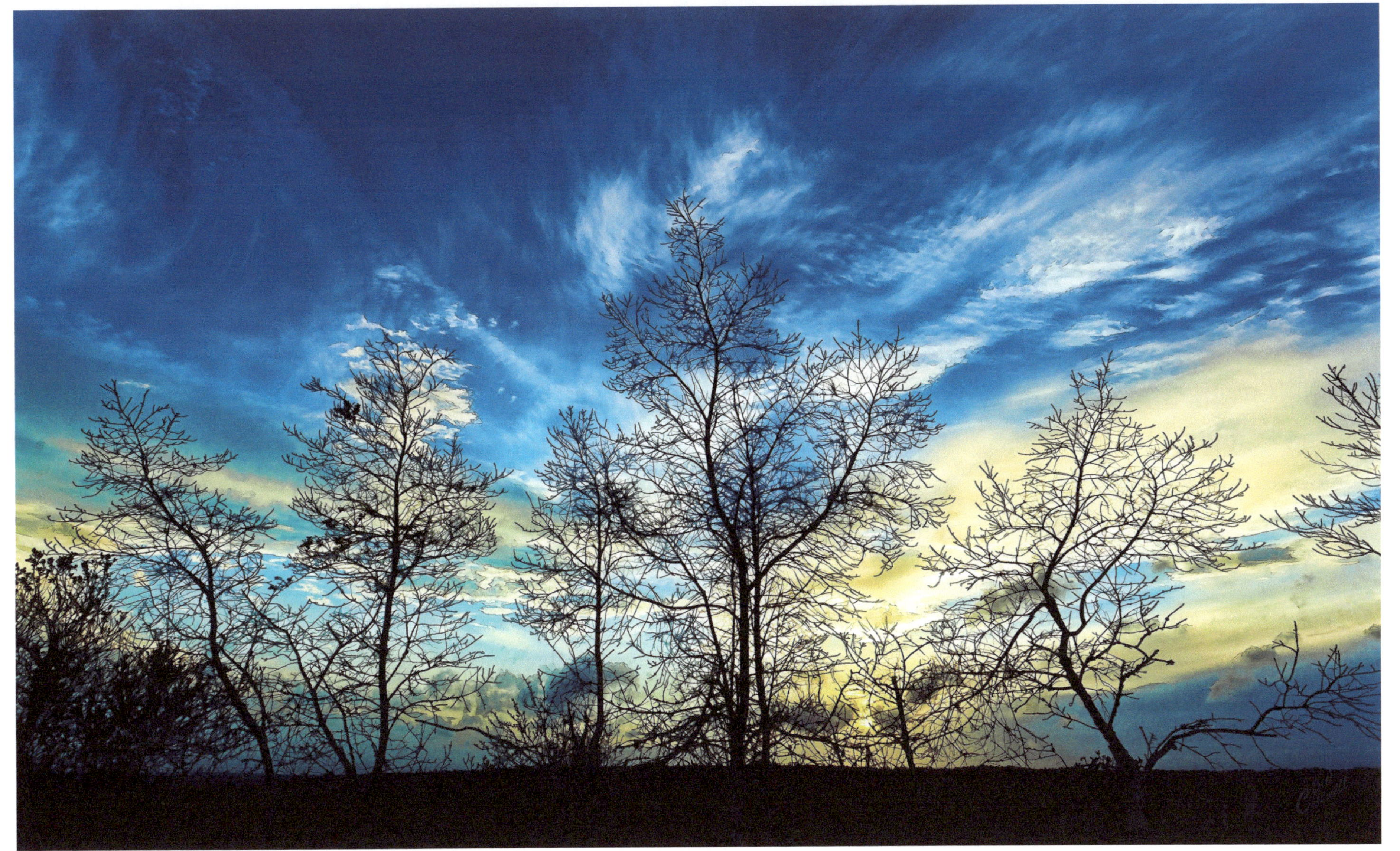

Letting Go

"The important thing is this: to be able, at any moment, to sacrifice what we are for what we could become."
— Maharishi Mahesh Yogi

Intention

An important part of walking a spiritual path is *intention*—a deliberate, conscious choice to follow a spiritual path. Intention is a powerful tool that sets the stage for forward movement, growth, and expansion. Intention lets the Universe know where you are at and where you want to go—that you're ready to move forward. Intention helps us live life deliberately, with awareness.

A few years ago I felt like I was becoming bogged down in my spiritual path and my art. About that same time I saw this blog on the Internet that mentioned a shamanic counselor and teacher, Clay Lomakayu, that lives in my area and helps people spiritually to "clear the way" so they can move forward. Although he does not consider himself to be a shaman, he says that he uses the methods of a shaman to help people. I found his website online, and his message and energy resonated with me. So I signed up for one of his intensive three-day sessions. This took a big leap of faith on my part because I had never done anything like this before. I had gone to a few group spiritual seminars before, but nothing this intense or personal. After 20 years in the Air Force, this was pretty far outside my comfort zone, but in my heart I knew this was something I needed to do. Using his shamanic methods, Clay is able to identify the rejected, hurt emotions that create blocks in your path. He doesn't necessarily identify the specific events, but rather the rejected emotions that surrounded those events. These rejected emotions have an energy of their own and the more we reject them, the more powerful they become, and the more they affect our lives in a negative way. By invoking these emotions in a very powerful way, Clay allows us to acknowledge those emotions and then let them go so they no longer block our way. I was amazed at how effective his methods were and how much lighter I felt afterward. Amazingly, the same week I scheduled this retreat, my website sold exactly enough pictures to pay for it. Was this just a coincidence or was the Universe responding to my *intent*—what Carlos Castaneda calls the active side of infinity? I, for one, don't believe it was just a coincidence.

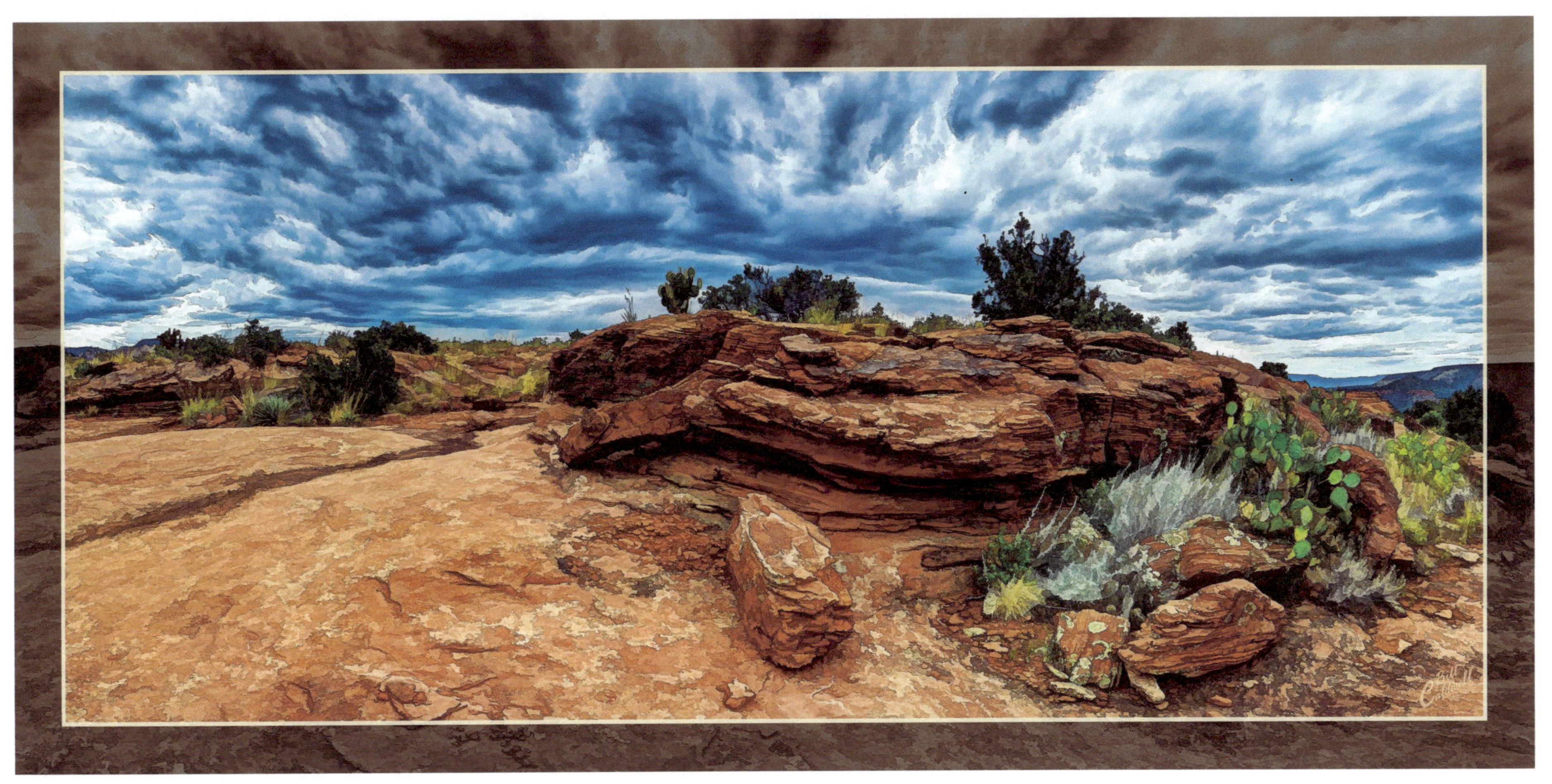

The Power of Intent

"In the universe there is an immeasurable, indescribable force which shamans call intent, and absolutely everything that exists in the entire cosmos is attached to intent by a connecting link."
— don Juan Matus (via Carlos Castaneda)

Vibrational Energy

"If you want to find the secrets of the universe, think in terms of energy, frequency and vibration."
— Nikola Tesla

When I was in high school, I took a physics class and learned the basics about vibrational energy which includes the electromagnetic spectrum as well as sound waves, earth quakes, and electricity. Physicists and medical researchers have discovered that absolutely everything in the physical world radiates some kind of vibrational energy including the human body; your brain, your heart, and even the thoughts that you think and the emotions that you feel. So when the Beach boys sing about "Good Vibrations," they're talking about something very real! And when spiritual teachers talk about raising your vibration, they too are talking about something very real. When you meet somebody for the first time and you have a good feeling about them, before they even say anything, this is your energy system sensing and reacting to their vibrational energy. Or when you meet somebody for the first time and you have a bad feeling about them, before they even start talking, then you know, once again, this is your energy system sensing and reacting to their vibrational energy. Where we get in trouble sometimes, is when we get this bad feeling about someone, but we ignore the feeling and listen to their words instead, which later turn out to be false or misleading. This is one reason why it's so important to listen to those subtle feelings that we have. The energy system that you are, is much deeper and more sensitive than the five physical senses. When we tune in to those deeper, more subtle feelings and intuition, then we begin to create what Gary Zukav calls "authentic power."

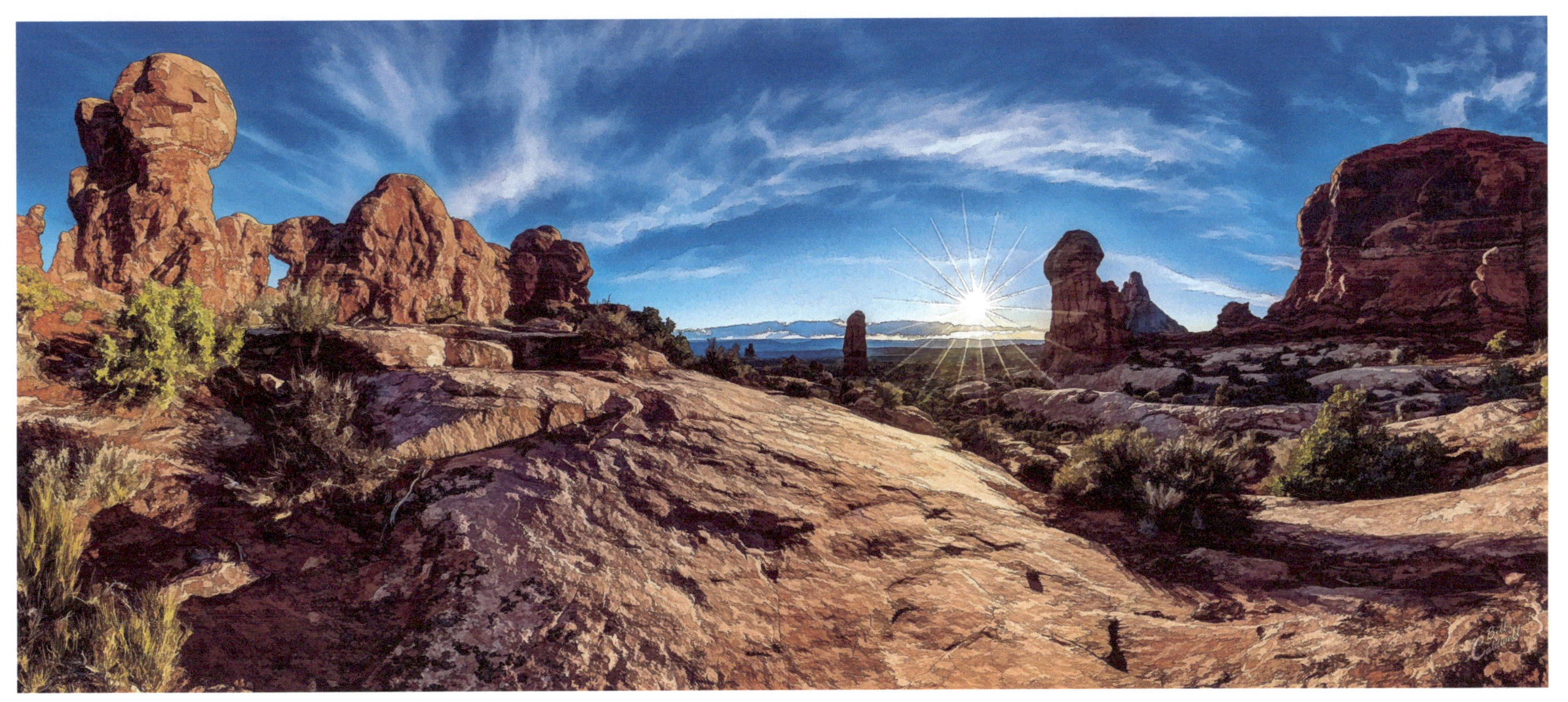

Arches Energy

"Concerning matter, we have been all wrong. What we have called matter is energy, whose vibration has been so lowered as to be perceptible to the senses. There is no matter."
— Albert Einstein

The people on this planet are beginning to understand the importance of light, energy, and vibration. Some are learning how to work with light, shapes, geometry, and energy to raise the vibrational energy of each atom and cell in their body to improve their physical and emotional well being—to come into vibrational harmony with their power. We can learn to do anything as long as we increase our own vibrational energy. Our thoughts need to be in alignment with those energies to be able to tap into the power that we all have and carry within us, the power we were born with. Because we don't currently believe we have this power, we aren't doing those things, but we *can* heal with touch. One of the things we absolutely must do—we must *believe* we can heal. And not just heal physically, but heal mentally, emotionally, and spiritually as well. As you believe you can heal, you move into alignment with those abilities and increase your vibrational energy so you can feel your power. Don't be afraid of your power. Most people fear their power, but it's all for good, and as you increase your energy, that vibrates out into the world, into the plants, the trees, the Earth, and even inanimate objects including our vehicles and our homes.

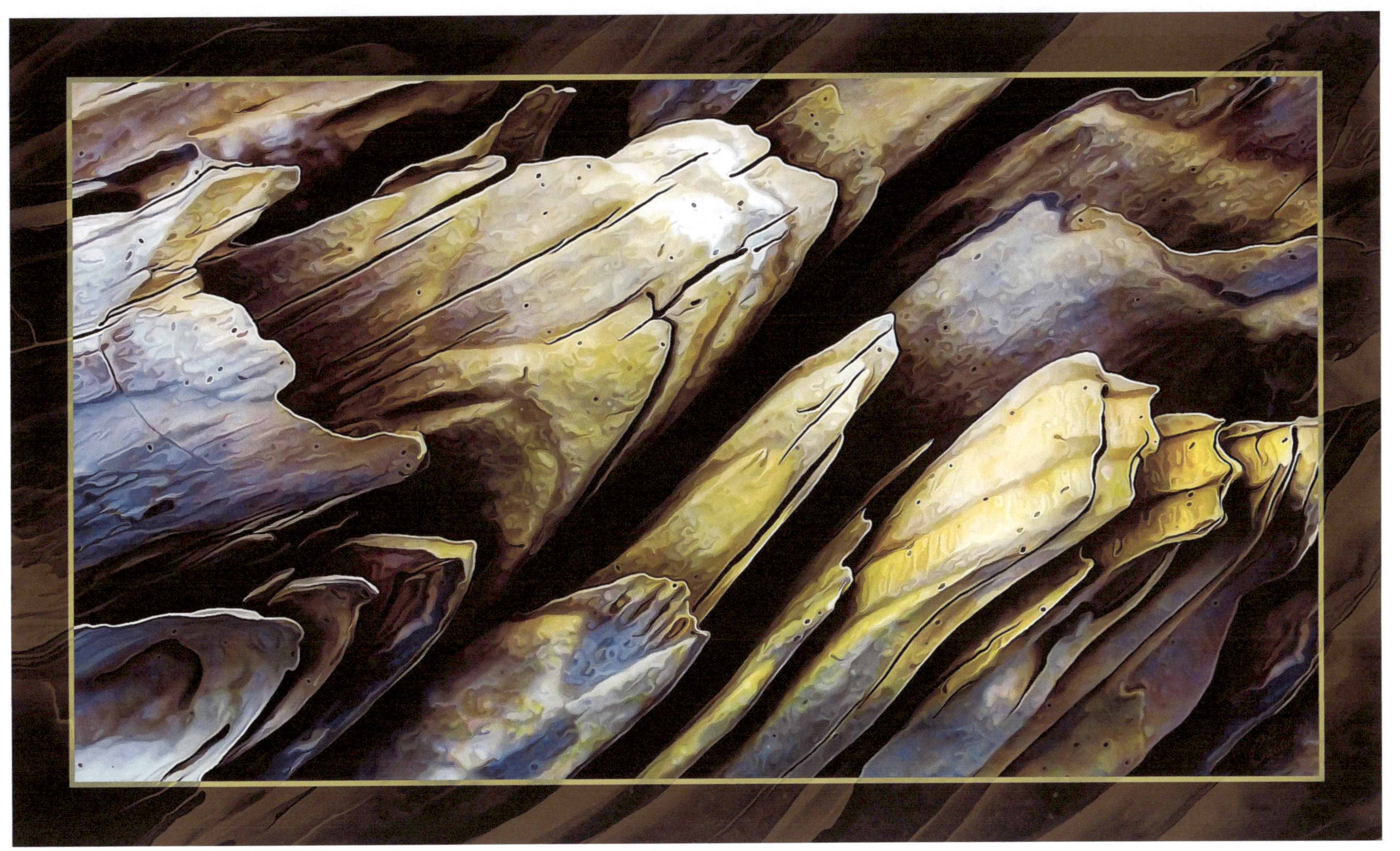

Driftwood Edges

*Everything is alive—everything has some level of consciousness. So start
seeing things as alive and having energy that can be increased in vibration.*

We can also use sound to increase our vibration, so be open to learning about this. For example, the sound of the word "Om" is very powerful. Different sounds have different vibrations, like humming or speaking in a different vibrational level with a different tone. Different tones will change the vibration. There are different ways to use sound, and things like singing bowls and musical instruments can be helpful, but these are not absolutely necessary because you can also use your own voices or focus on the sounds around you. The sounds of nature are very beneficial; the sound of a babbling brook, waves at the beach, birds singing, the purring of a cat, the muffled silence when the air is filled with mist. And small changes are important—every little thing that raises the vibration of one person or a group of people benefits many. These things are important to know because it helps raise the vibration of Earth so the Earth becomes a better place and a better planet, and this will increase the vibrational energy of our universe. And the more universes that have positive energy, the better it is for every living creature everywhere!

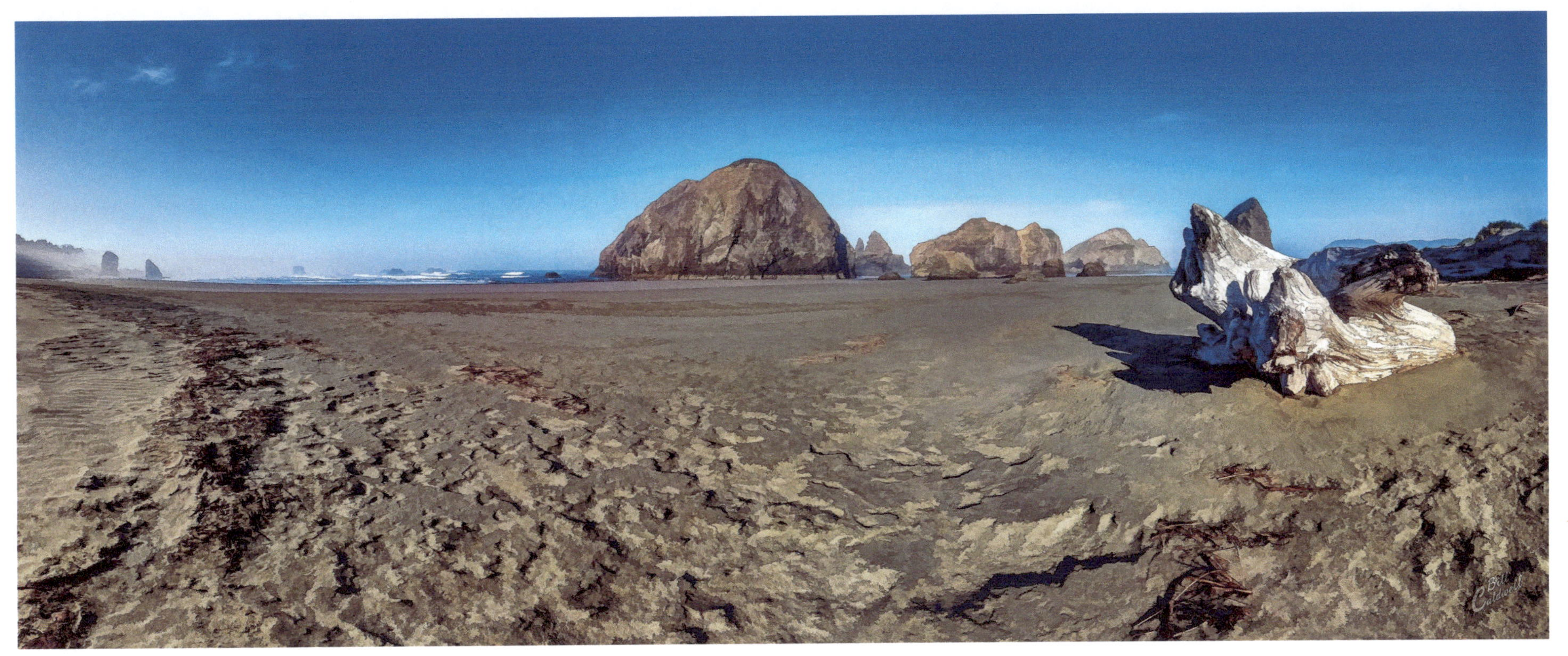

Earth Energy

Small changes are important.
Every little thing that raises the vibration of one person or a group of people benefits many.
The more positive energy vibrating through the universe, the better it is for every living creature everywhere!

There is no Death

There is no death. We are here in the "Earth School Simulator" to learn, to grow, to expand our awareness, to expand our consciousness, and to increase our understanding of ourselves and the Universe. And when we reach the end of our physical life, we transition to the nonphysical world, a kind of graduation, a celebration of the lessons we learned and the advances we made. To me, physical life is similar to an aircraft simulator. When I was in the Air Force, part of my training involved the use of an aircraft simulator. The whole idea of a simulator is that, while you're in the simulator, everything looks the same as a real aircraft. Everything functions, sounds, and feels real. With a little imagination, it feels like you're actually flying an airplane. When you're in the simulator you never actually leave the ground of course, so if you make any mistakes or there's an emergency and you end up crashing, you don't actually crash. So now you can figure out what happened and learn from that experience, unharmed. To me, this physical life that we're all experiencing is like the aircraft simulator in the sense that everything seems very real—as if this physical life is all there is. So when something happens or old age causes someone's physical body to stop functioning, it seems to the rest of us as if that person ceases to exist. In reality, your spirit or soul, Who-You-Really-Are, is unharmed. You simply return to the nonphysical realm to review the lessons you learned and to plan your next physical life in the Earth School Simulator. And once the soul moves on from the physical world, it should not be portrayed as indifferent. Those who have transitioned to the nonphysical still care about us and want to help in our growth. Know that you are not forgotten. Souls are always growing and expanding in both the physical and nonphysical realm and we are all part of that expansion in some capacity.

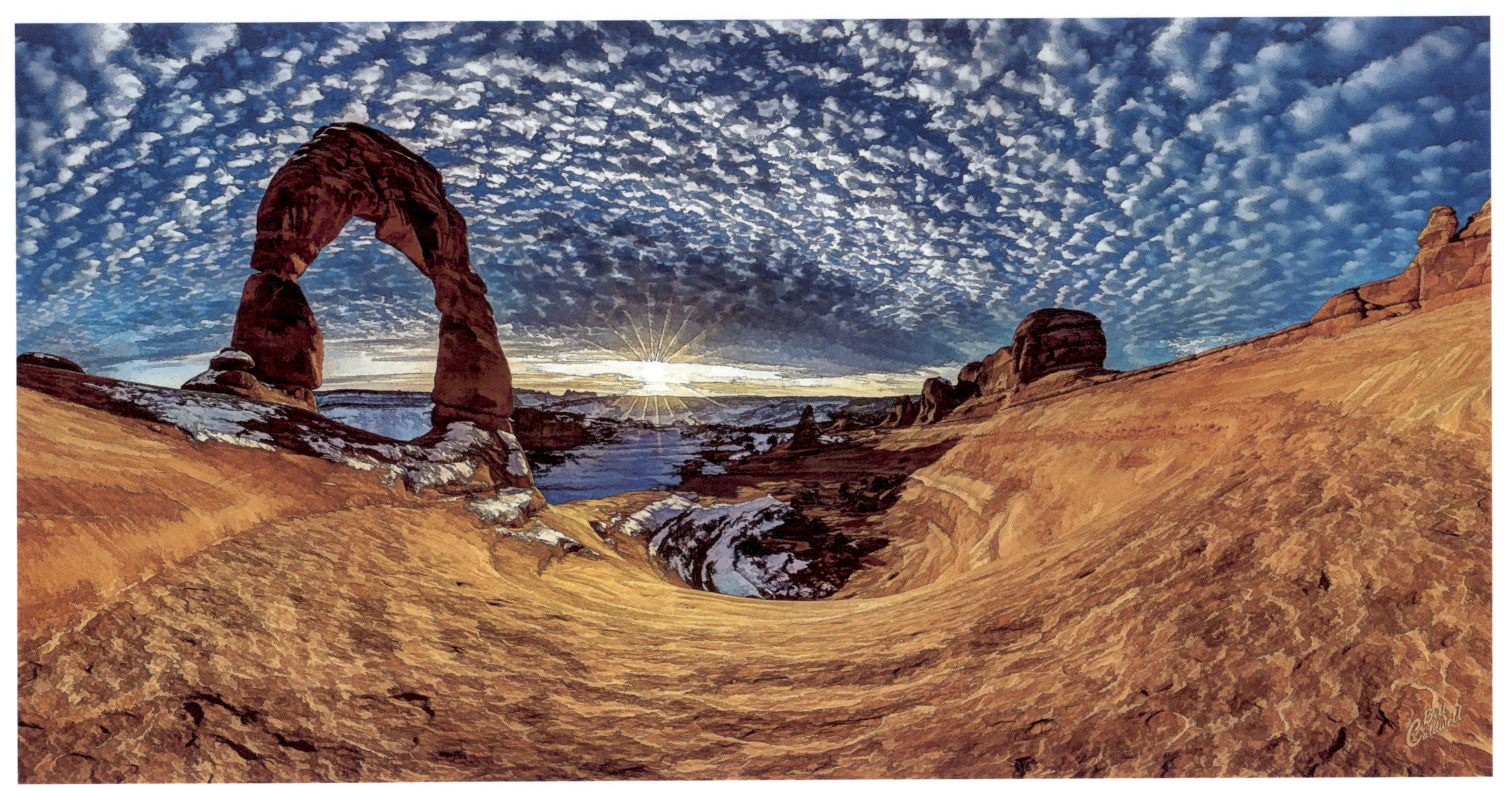

Radiant Gateway

"Death is a fiction, it doesn't exist. It can't occur in the experience of who you are, which is a Sacred Being known as your Soul that lives past what you call the end of your physical life. Why would you be sad if someone has celebrated their Continuation Day? Death is never an end, but always a beginning. A death is a door opening, not a door closing." — Neale Donald Walsch

The first time I read about the idea of reincarnation and past lives was when I was in junior high school and I read Paramahansa Yogananda's book "Autobiography of a Yogi." At first I wasn't really sure intellectually about this idea, but it sounded true and resonated with me. Of course, many of the world's major religions believe in some sort of soul and some sort of life after death, but they don't all believe that the soul incarnates in multiple physical lives. As I continue to read various books throughout my life, my belief in multiple physical lives has become strengthened. This belief truly resonates with me and, to me, it makes perfect sense. The book that really brought it home for me was "Many Lives, Many Masters" by Dr. Brian Weiss, as well as his other books that followed. As it turns out, past life regression therapy is very effective at alleviating psychological issues that are resistant to traditional psychotherapy. We are affected by our other lives, both past and future, in both positive ways and negative ways. Sometimes past life traumas are carried into our current life, giving us emotional challenges that we have to overcome. In addition, our spiritual growth in each of our physical lives helps all of our incarnations. We are all on a journey of spiritual growth and expansion, and this occurs through the incarnation of many physical lives, as well as our experiences in the nonphysical realm between physical lives. We are all eternal spiritual beings and our lives, our spirit, our souls, that is to say Who-You-Really-Are, never ends. Our path of growth and expansion is eternal and timeless. There will always be something new to learn, to discover, and to understand.

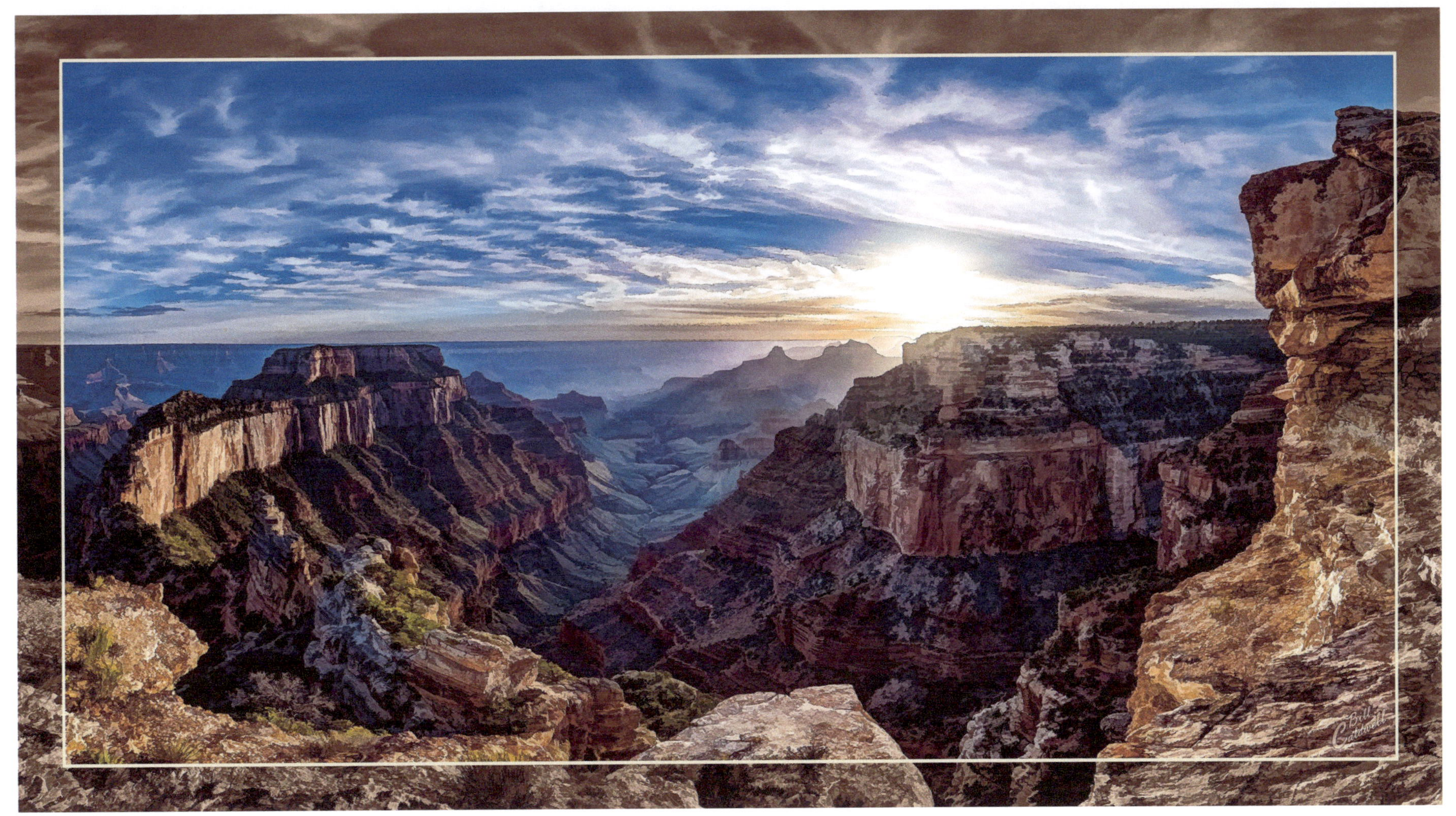

Eternal Transformation

"When we get to the spiritual plane, we keep growing there too. We decide when we want to return, where, and for what reasons. Some choose not to come back. They choose to go on to another stage of development. And they stay in spirit form…some for longer than others before they return. It is all growth and learning…continuous growth. Our body is just a vehicle for us while we're here. It is our soul and our spirit that last forever." — Dr. Brian Weiss

Something to Think About

"I shall not commit the fashionable stupidity of regarding everything I cannot explain as a fraud."
— Carl Jung

These are things I've learned and come to believe that may be difficult to believe or difficult to understand from the limited perspective of our physical human lives. In order to accept these ideas, I had to let go of certain attitudes and beliefs that were part of the mental conditioning of my upbringing and education. From the perspective of the Universe, we are still just infants in our understanding of who we really are and how the Universe works. Please keep an open mind as you read these ideas. Some may resonate with you and others may not. Either way, it's OK. As Sylvia Brown often said: "Take what you like and leave the rest."

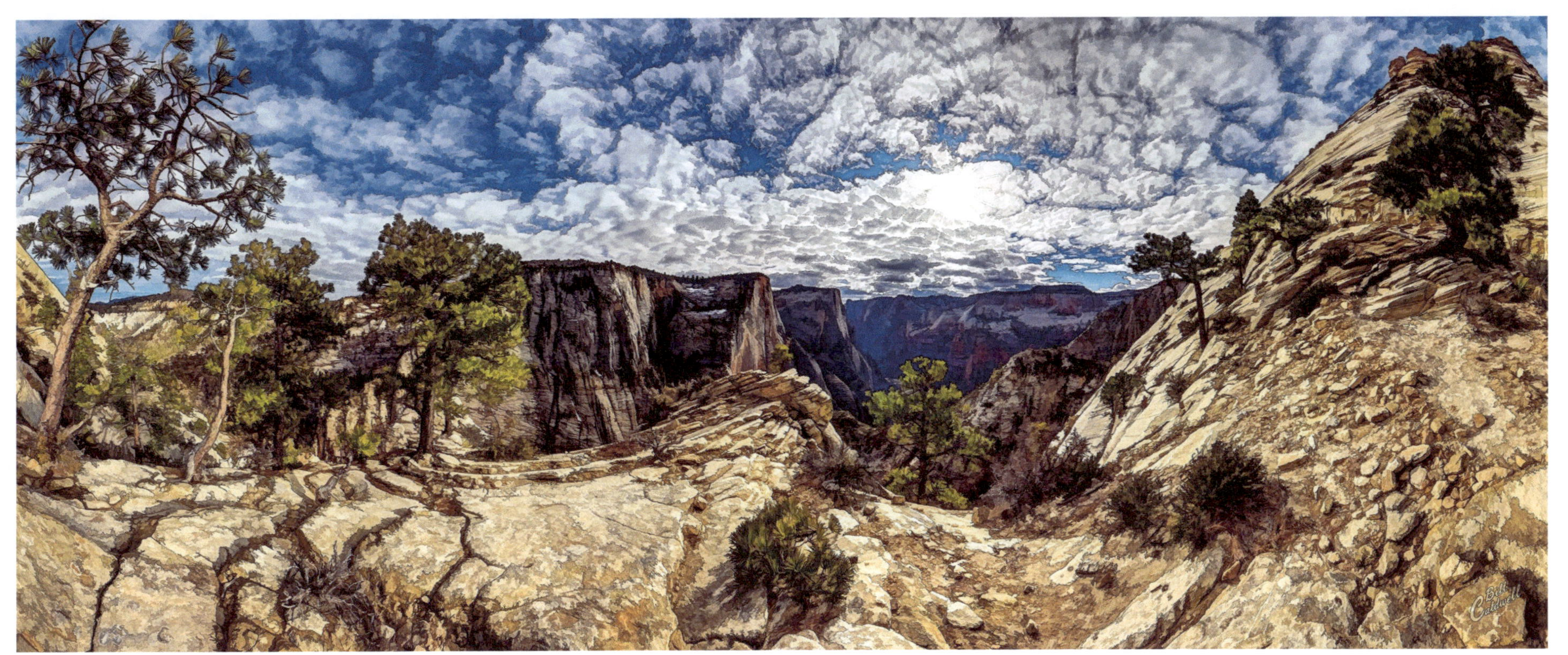

The Awakening

When you begin to awaken, and the truth resonates in your heart and soul, you begin to realize that what you once believed, what you were taught to be true, may simply be a misunderstanding or misinterpretation of those who came before us.

Although our astronomers have shown us that our physical universe is incredibly large, with billions of galaxies containing billions of stars, this is still just a limited view. Actually, our universe is unlimited. And if that doesn't blow your mind, there are an unlimited number of other universes, and all this exists in a framework of unlimited dimensions.

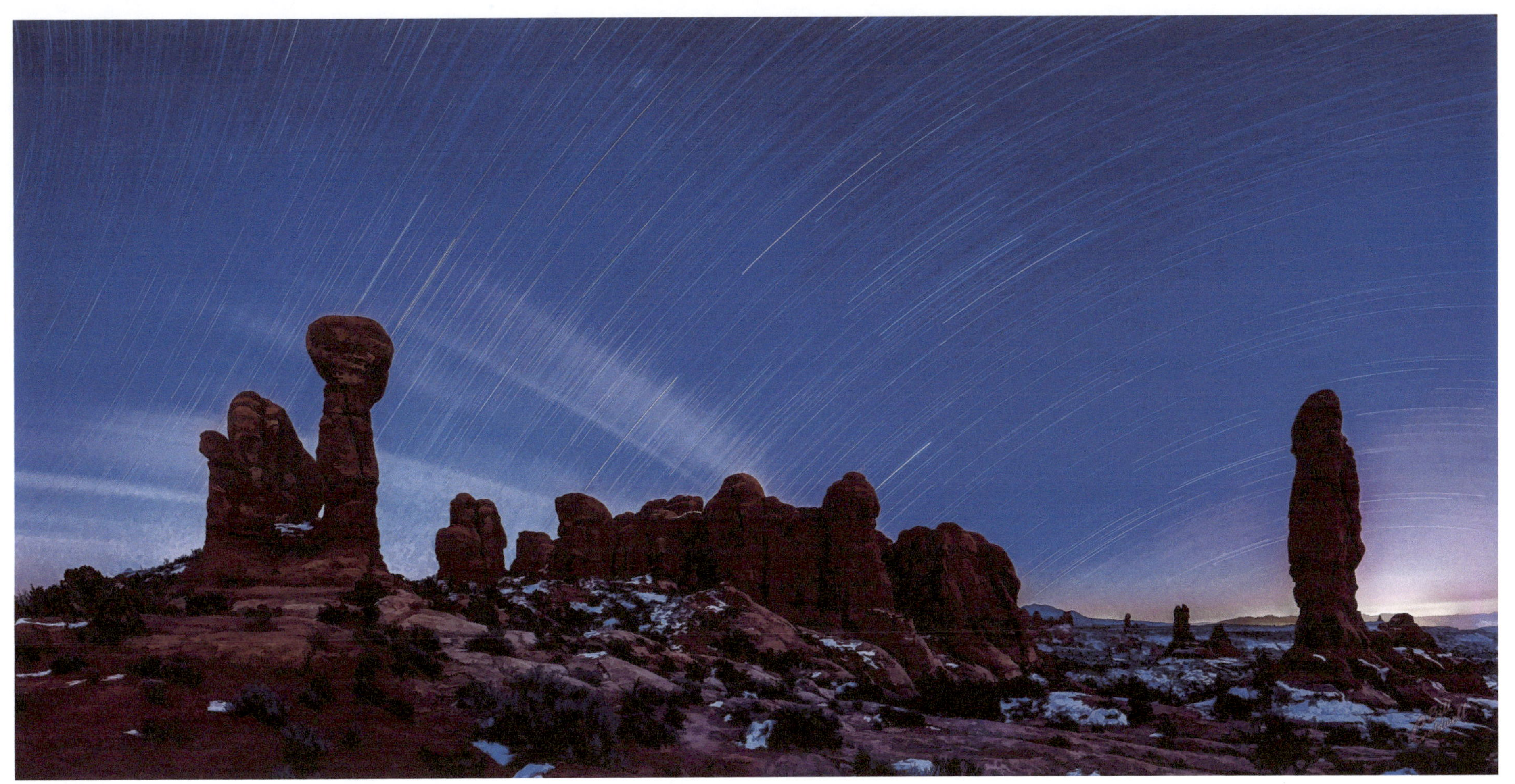

A Conscious Universe

*The more you learn about yourself, about Who-You-Really-Are and the gifts you have to share,
the more you benefit and the more the whole Universe benefits.*

Souls often reincarnate in groups that have shared past life experiences, as family members or other relationships. But this is not always the case. Sometimes individual souls are born into families with no shared past life experiences. These individuals may not feel a strong connection to their biological family members in the way that many other people do. This is sometimes necessary so that later in life, they meet certain people, make connections, and have experiences that are important for the growth and expansion of their soul. I was about 7 years old when my siblings and I moved to live with our dad and our stepmom Chris. I felt an immediate, strong connection with Chris and I now know that I've shared past lives with her. For me, she was a godsend. She had a huge positive affect on my life. I met my wife later in life, when I was 28, and as it turns out, we've had many other lives together and she has been a very important part of my spiritual growth and expansion.

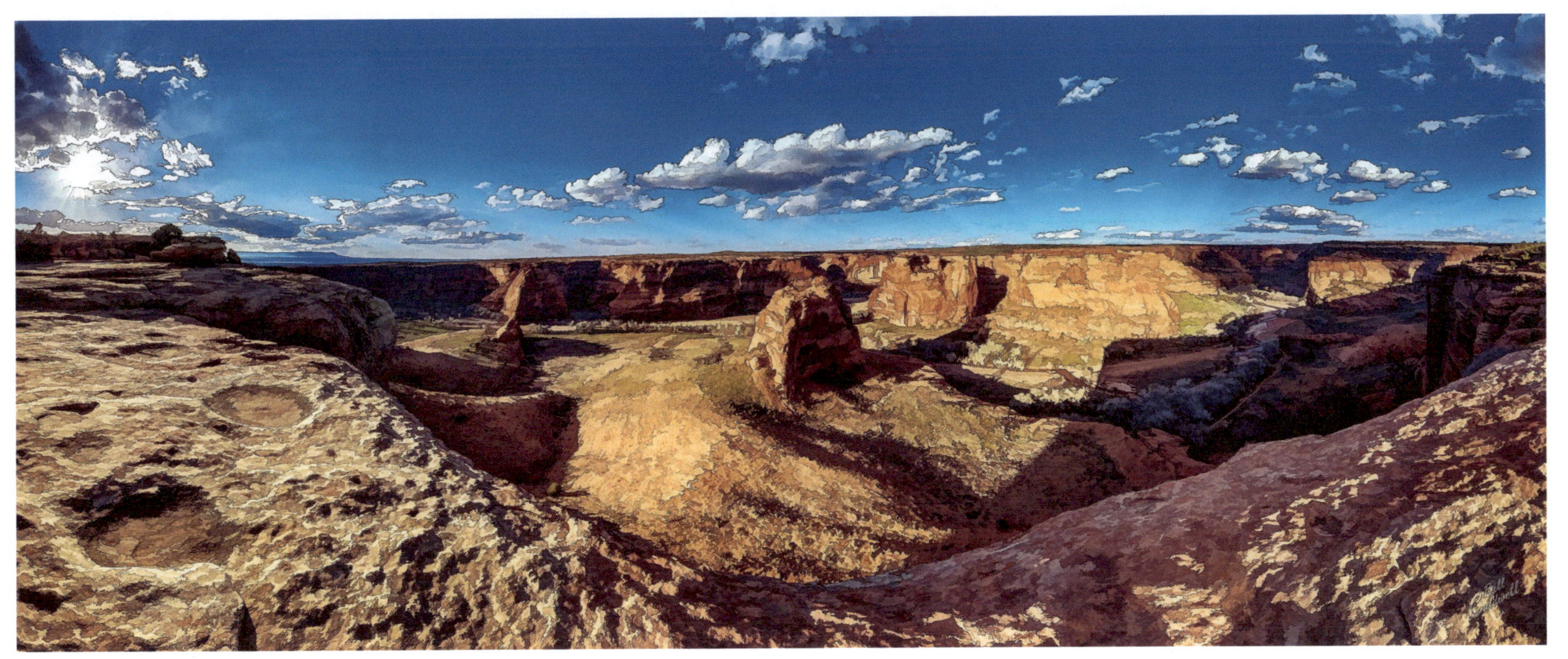

One Enduring Soul

"To see and appreciate the soul of others with whom you are in a relationship is a higher state of awareness. To see only their outer characteristics provides a limited and incomplete perspective. Their current personality, just like their current physical body, is a temporary manifestation. They have had many bodies and many personalities but only one enduring soul, only one continuous spiritual essence. See this essence and you will see the real person." — Dr. Brian Weiss

The greater part of Who-You-Really-Are, your nonphysical being or soul, is way too large to fit into a single physical body, so the greater part of it stays in the nonphysical/spiritual realm. Only small parts of our higher self or soul enter into physical bodies, and we can, and do, incarnate in many different physical forms concurrently in various locations, dimensions, and universes. Often times what we think of as past lives are actually simultaneous lives. And all of these separate lives are connected metaphysically to each other through our higher self, Source, and all other beings. The spiritual growth and expansion that each individual experiences affects and helps every other individual, "past, present, and future."

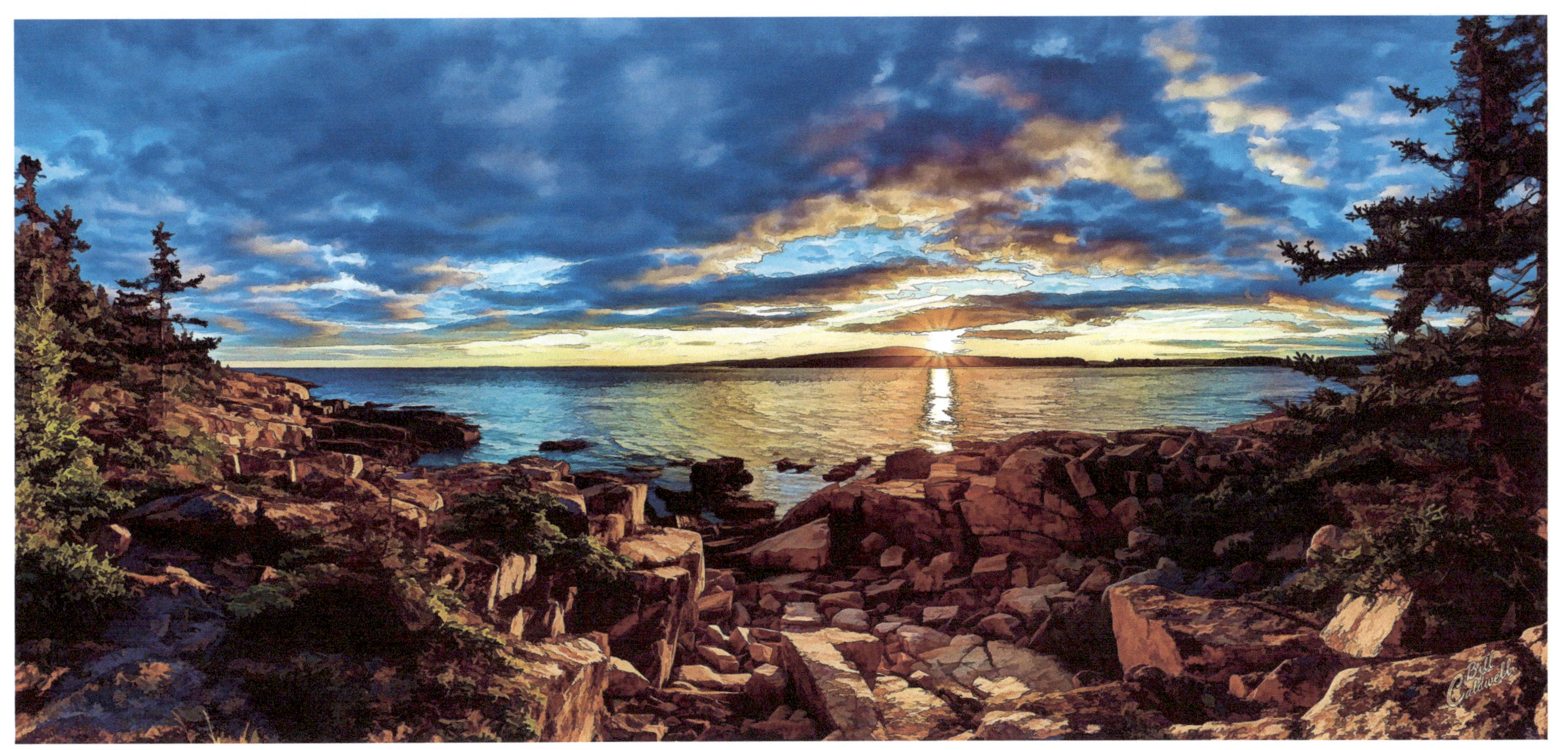

Point of View

"From the point of view of the soul, all of its incarnations are simultaneous. All of its personalities exist at once. Therefore, the release of negativity that occurs in one of the soul's incarnations benefits not only itself, but all of its soul's other incarnations also." — Gary Zukav

From the perspective of our physical human form, we have a very limited concept of time. For us, time appears to be linear; moving from a past that seems to be gone, to the present, to a future that does not seem to exist yet. From the perspective of the Universe, past, present, and future exist simultaneously, like the folds in a Japanese fan or the layers of an onion.

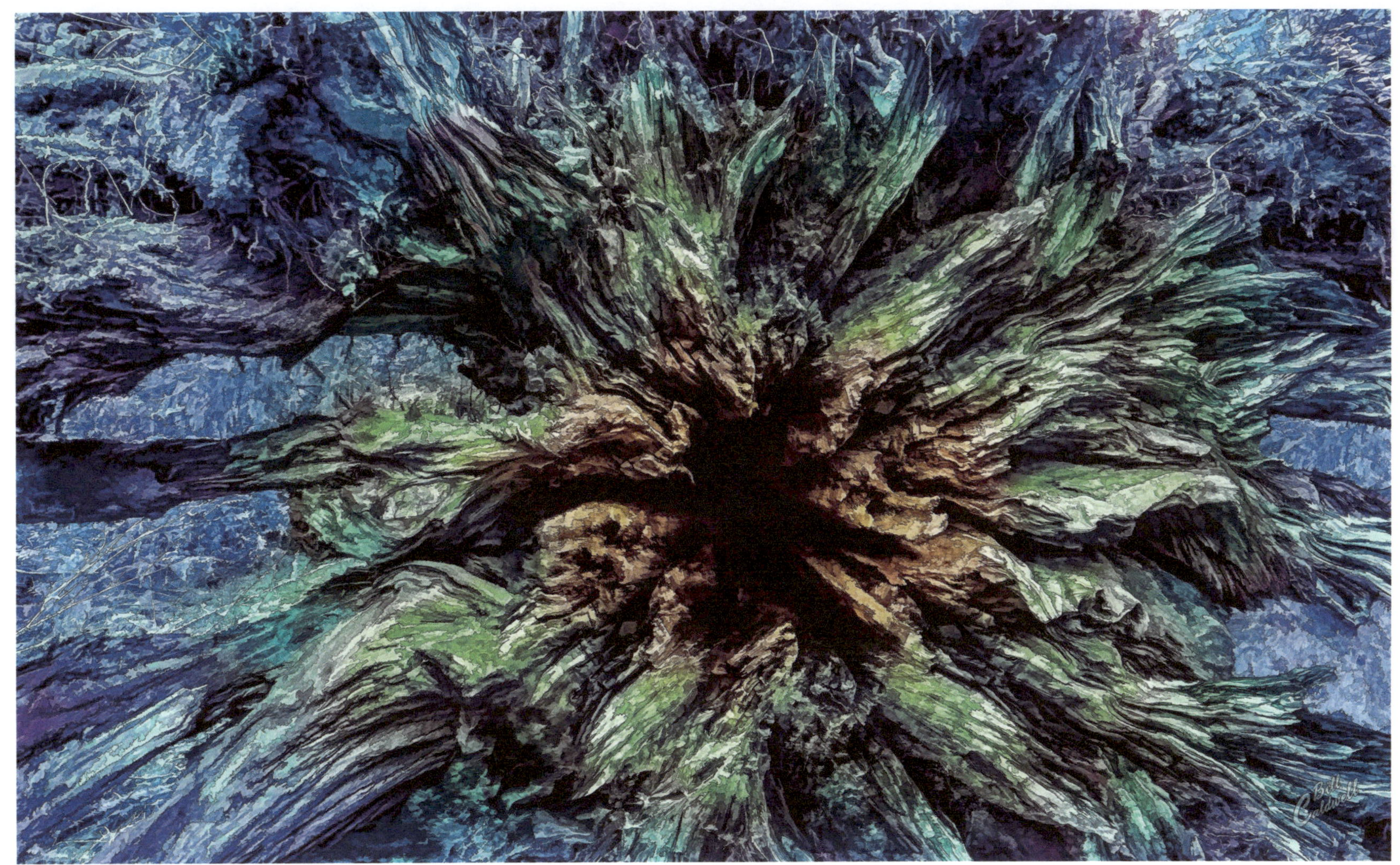

Expansion

"Before the contrast and before the summoning, and before the answering of Source Energy, the Universe was less. So rather than thinking in terms of time, think in terms of expansion, and then you will understand time in the way we understand it. We never think about how long anything takes. We are just enjoying the expansion. And so, our now is always powerful in our anticipation of what is becoming." — Abraham-Hicks

The physical universe is filled with life. Every planet and every conceivable environment has life of some kind. It may not be in a form that humans will recognize, it may not fit the rules of biology that our scientists understand, but life exists in every nook and cranny of the universe. All the various planets and environments have different physical forms, and different chemical and biological characteristics, based on the evolution of the planet itself. The life forms that live there are suited to that environment, and may evolve as the planet evolves.

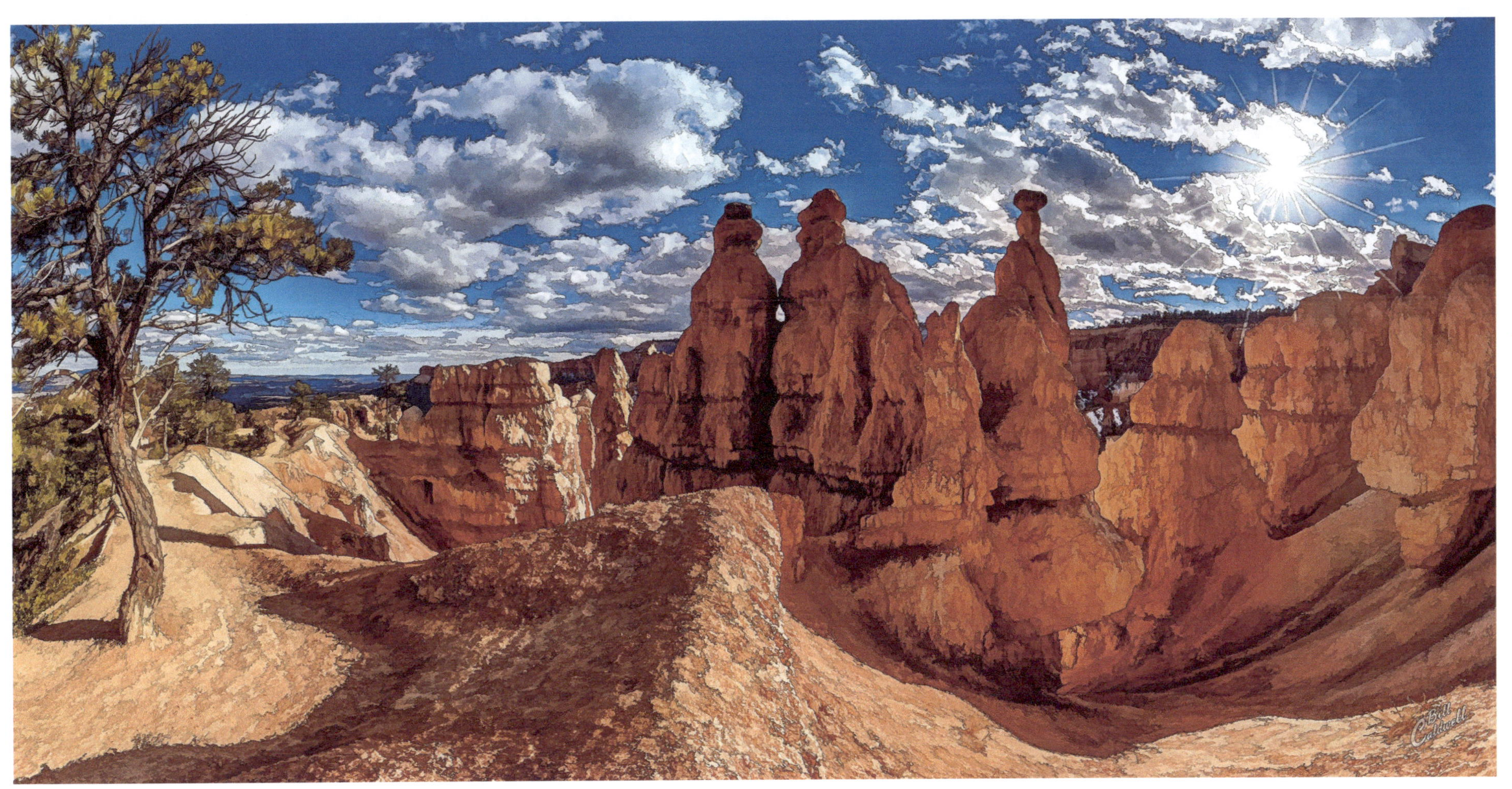

The Guardians

"Every physical form, as well as every nonphysical form, is Light that has been shaped by consciousness. No form exists apart from consciousness. There is not one planet in the universe that does not have an active level of consciousness, although it may not be what we recognize." — Gary Zukav

What if we could travel to other planets, solar systems, or galaxies without having to use a spaceship? There are many Portals and Gateways scattered throughout the universe, linked together in a massive network that allows beings to travel to various places and times. The stars and planets go through evolutionary processes and sometimes go through extreme, cataclysmic changes. This is part of their journey of growth, expansion, and evolution. Before planets go through major cataclysmic changes and expansions, like the earth did 65 million years ago when the dinosaurs disappeared, the beings that live on that planet are given the opportunity to be transported to new worlds and, if necessary, their physical makeup is transformed at the molecular level so they can live in that new environment.

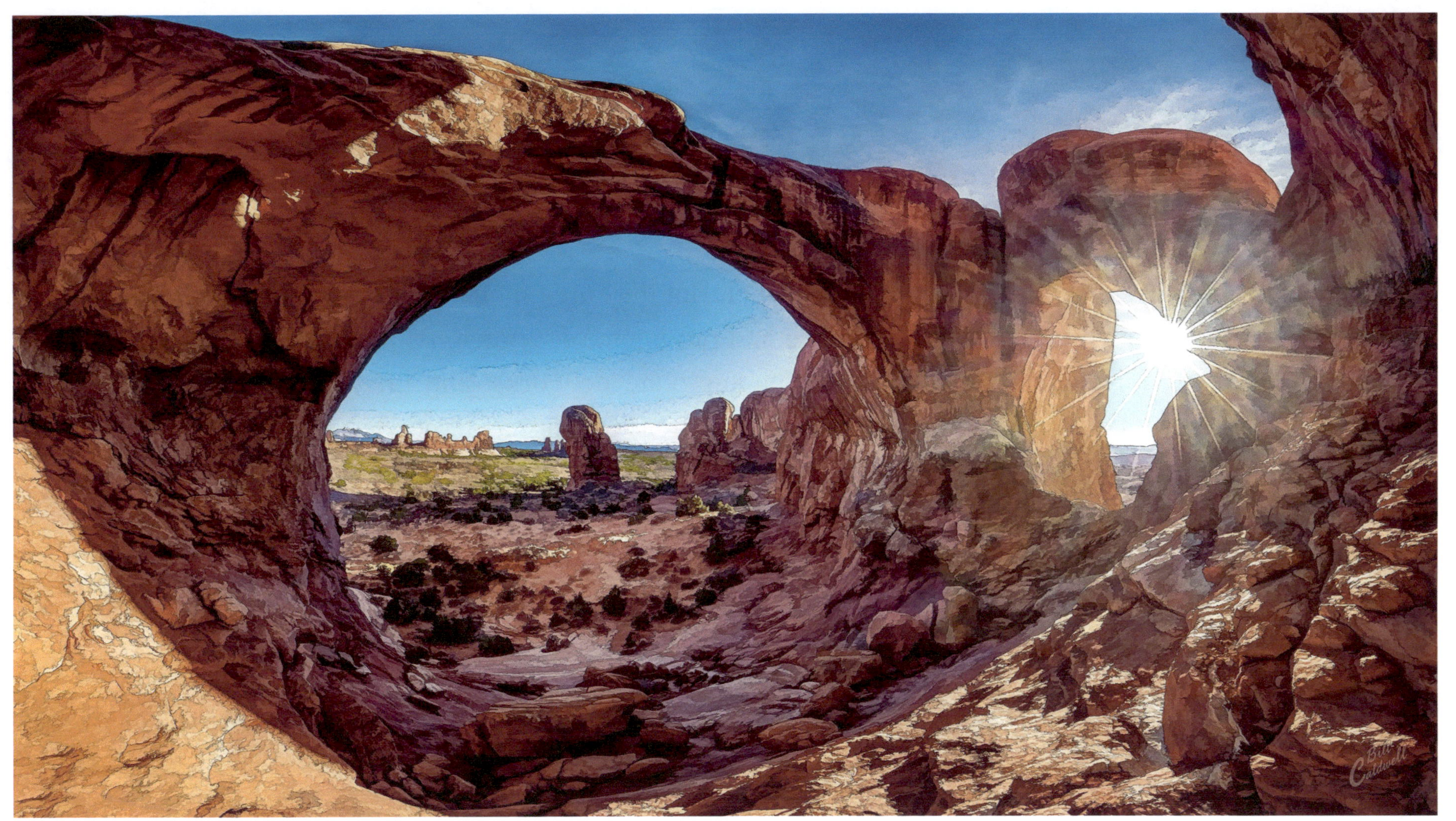

Ancient Portal

"There comes a time when the mind takes a higher plane of knowledge, but can never prove how it got there."
– Albert Einstein

Trees are absolutely essential for life on this planet. But they are much more than just providers of habitat, much more than just converters of carbon dioxide and providers of oxygen. Although they appear to be lone individuals, they are connected through massive underground networks, and the greater part of their being lives underground. Trees are ancient sentient beings with great wisdom and knowledge that they would like to share with us if we are able to open our hearts, still our thinking minds, and listen. And just like the trees, we are all connected through an unseen metaphysical network of energy, so we are never really alone.

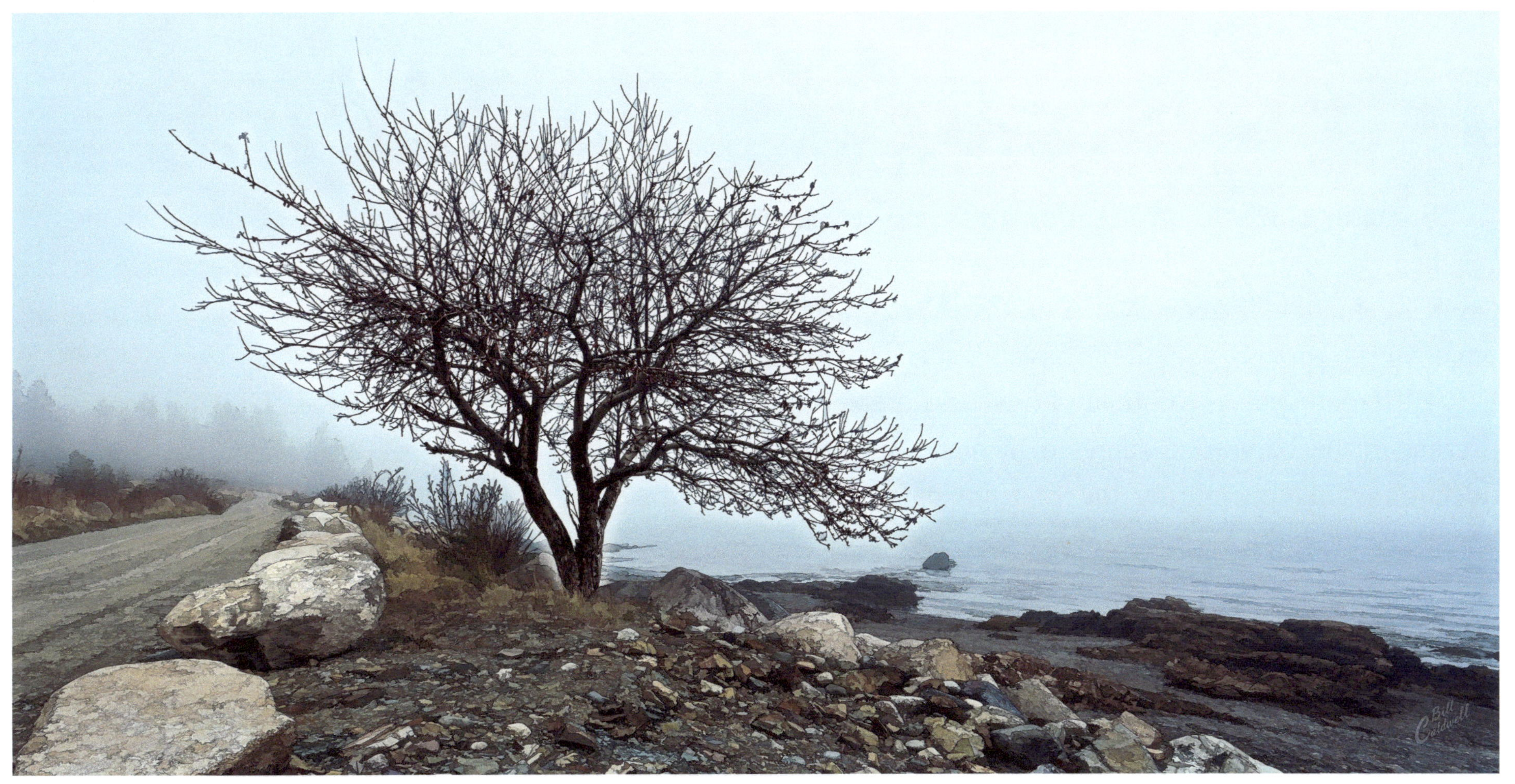

The Sentinel

Trees are ancient sentient beings with great wisdom and knowledge that they would like to share. Clear your mind of thoughts, open your heart, and try to listen.

Sometimes whole species of beings choose to leave the planet because conditions are no longer conducive for their continued well being. There are many examples of this on Earth including the Passenger Pigeon, Sea Mink, Tasmanian Tiger, Great Auk, Caribbean Monk Seal, and many others. Many of these recent departures, what we refer to as extinctions, have been caused by the pressures of human activity.

Different species of beings have different vibrational energy levels and patterns. Certain beings are present in the beginning stages of a planet and are there to protect and shape the vibrational energy of the developing planet. During the lifespan of a planet, many different life forms come and go as the planet changes and evolves.

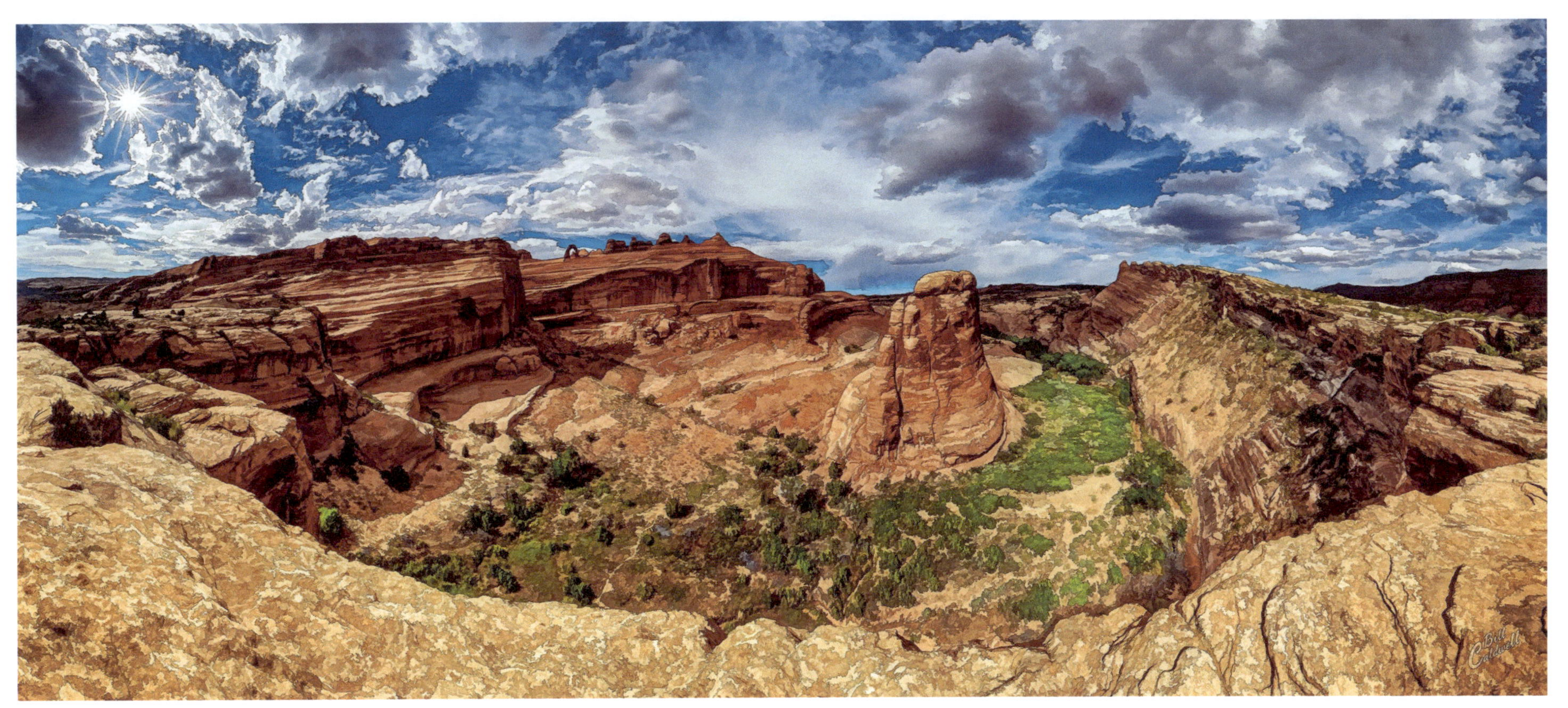

The End of the Beginning

"Just as each person's soul grows through the hurdles and challenges of life, humanity is meant to face these challenges together, all to catalyze our growth to unprecedented levels. We have much cause for hope—that a brilliant and harmonious future can be ours. As more of us come to know that truly we are all eternal spiritual beings, the world will become far more harmonious and peaceful." —Dr. Eben Alexander

There are many life forms on Earth that humans are not aware of or don't recognize as such. Many of these live deep underground or deep beneath the oceans and some have been driven deep into the mountains and forests, seldom or never to be seen.

None of the life forms on Earth originated on this planet—they all came from somewhere else. And all of them are connected metaphysically to kindred beings on other planets or in other universes. This concept becomes easier to embrace once you accept that we are not alone in the universe.

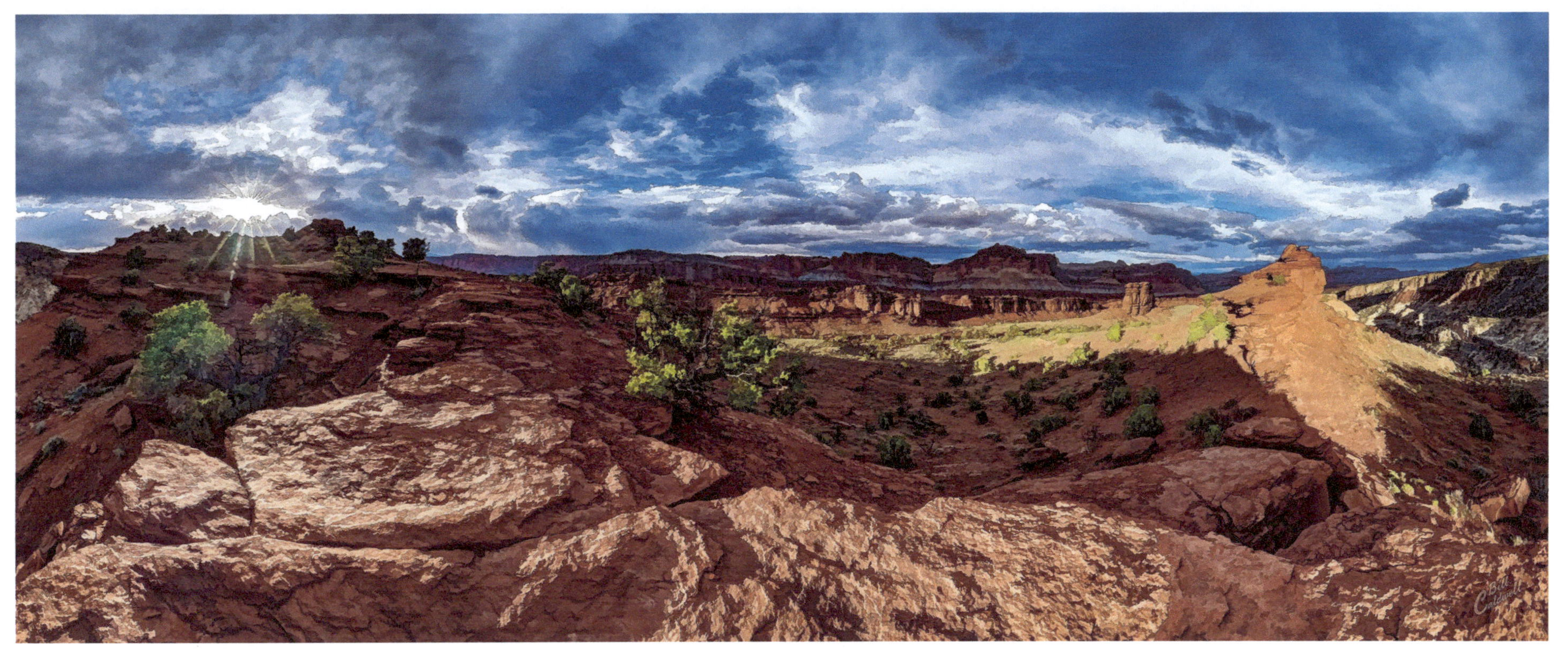

Infinite Possibilities

The universe is truly amazing and limitless. Anything your mind can imagine is possible and may already exist somewhere in the universe—the possibilities are infinite!

If there's anything I've learned during my life, it's that there is much more going on in the world and the universe than meets the eye. Much more going on than our five senses or scientific instruments will show us, much more than any religion will tell us, much more than most people are aware of or can imagine. The universe is a fantastic and mysterious place.

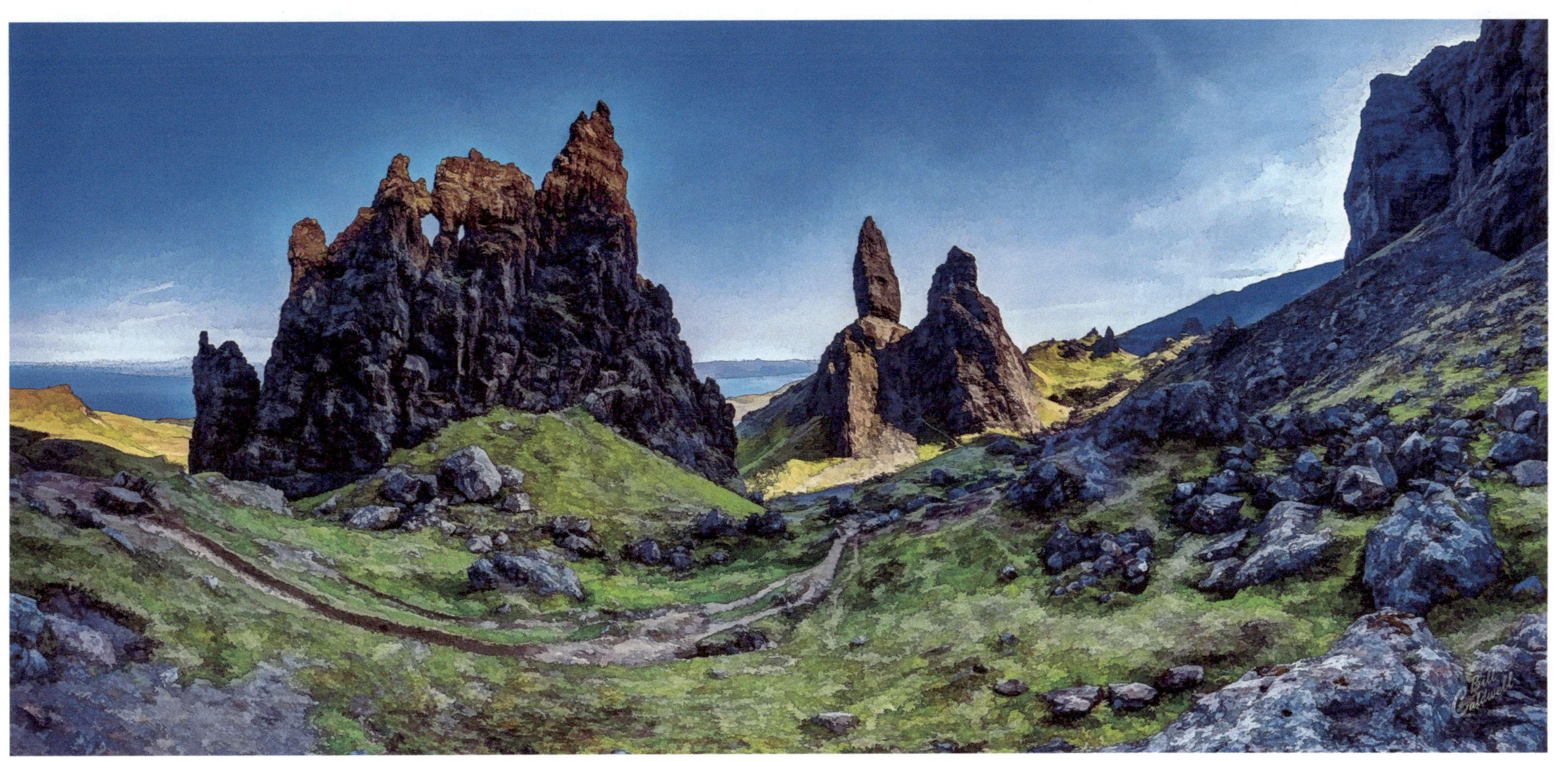

The Timeless Path

We are all eternal spiritual beings and our lives, our spirit, our souls, that is to say Who-You-Really-Are, never ends. Our path of growth and expansion is eternal and timeless. There will always be something new to learn, to discover, and to understand.

What If

What if all people from all lands worked together in cooperation and collaboration?

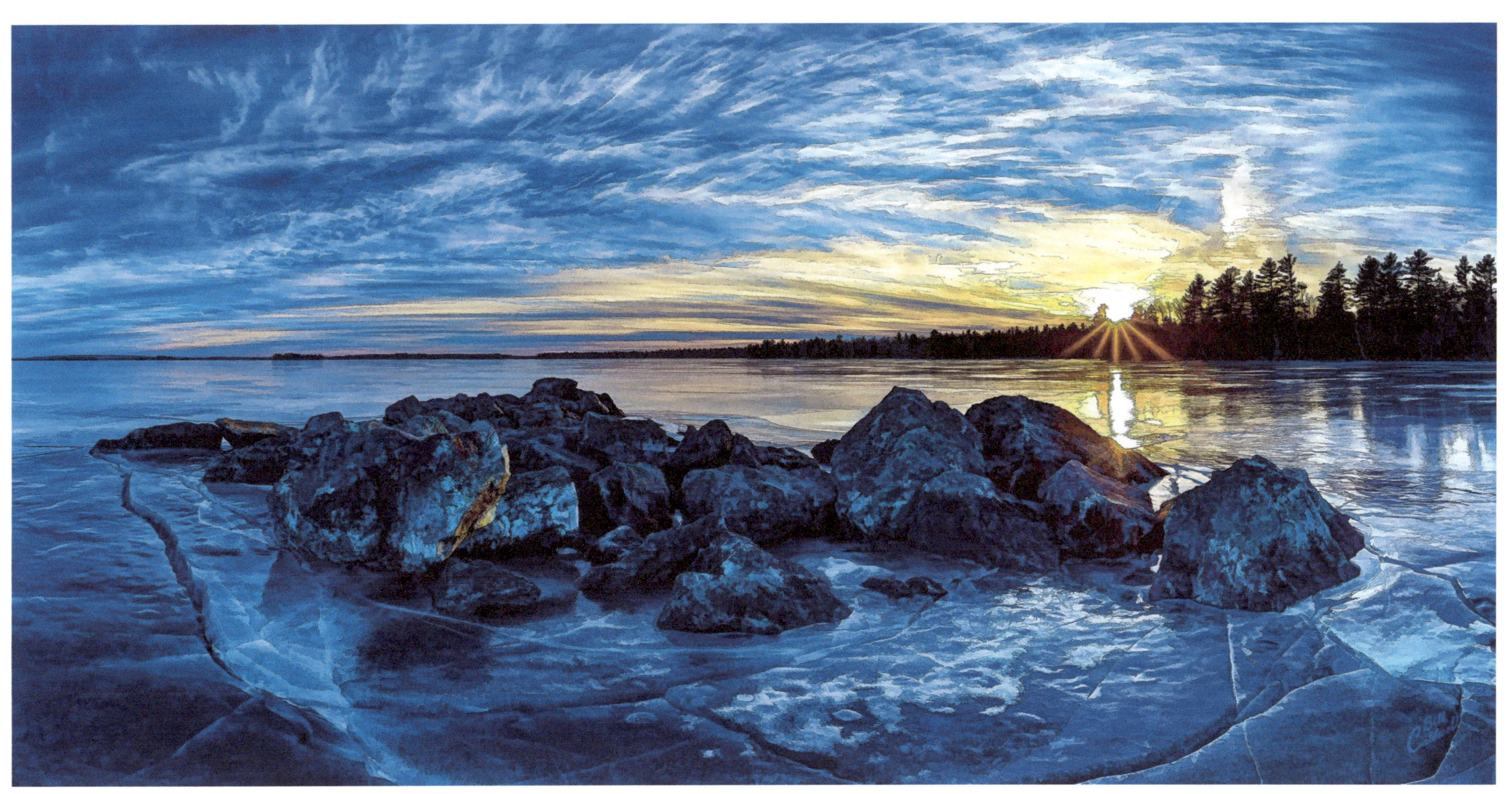

Synergy

What if we all set aside our political and religious differences and worked together for the benefit of all?

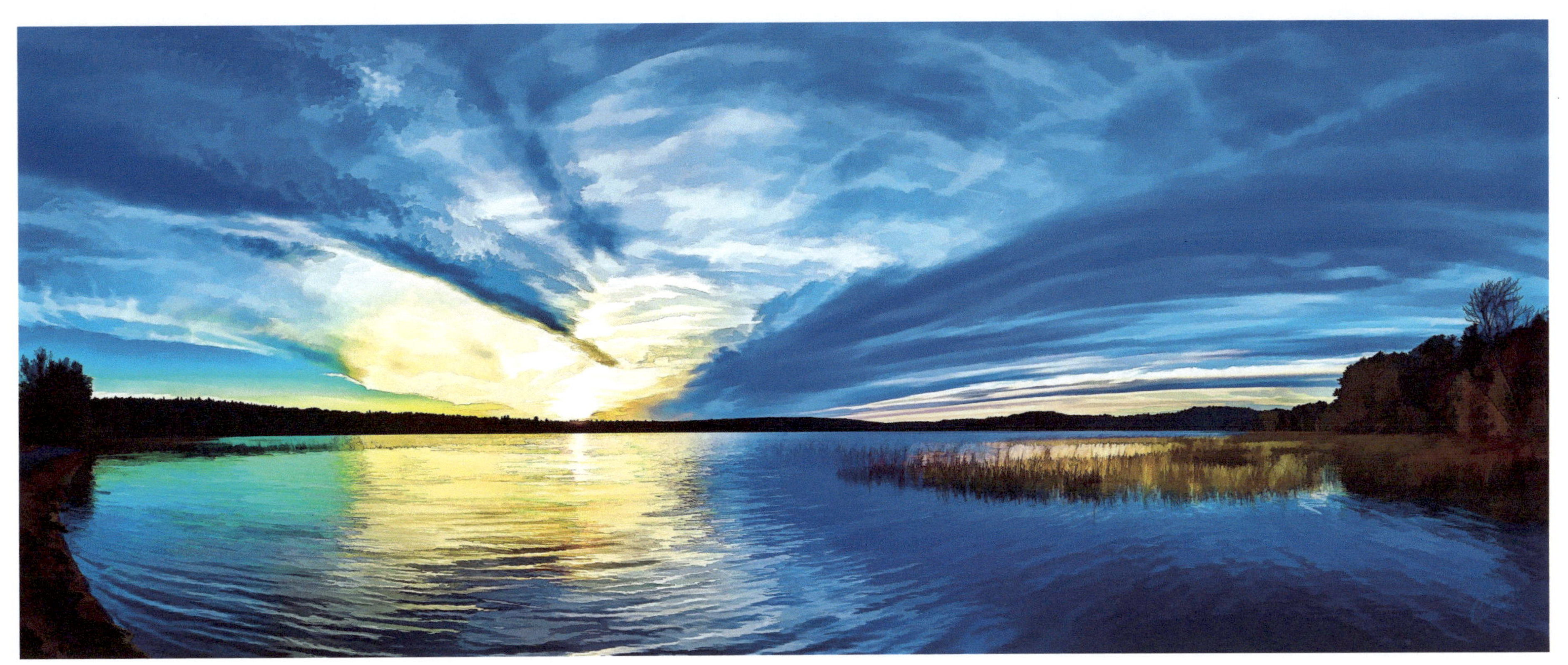

For the Benefit of All

What if we all set aside our self-interest and hubris and made responsible choices?

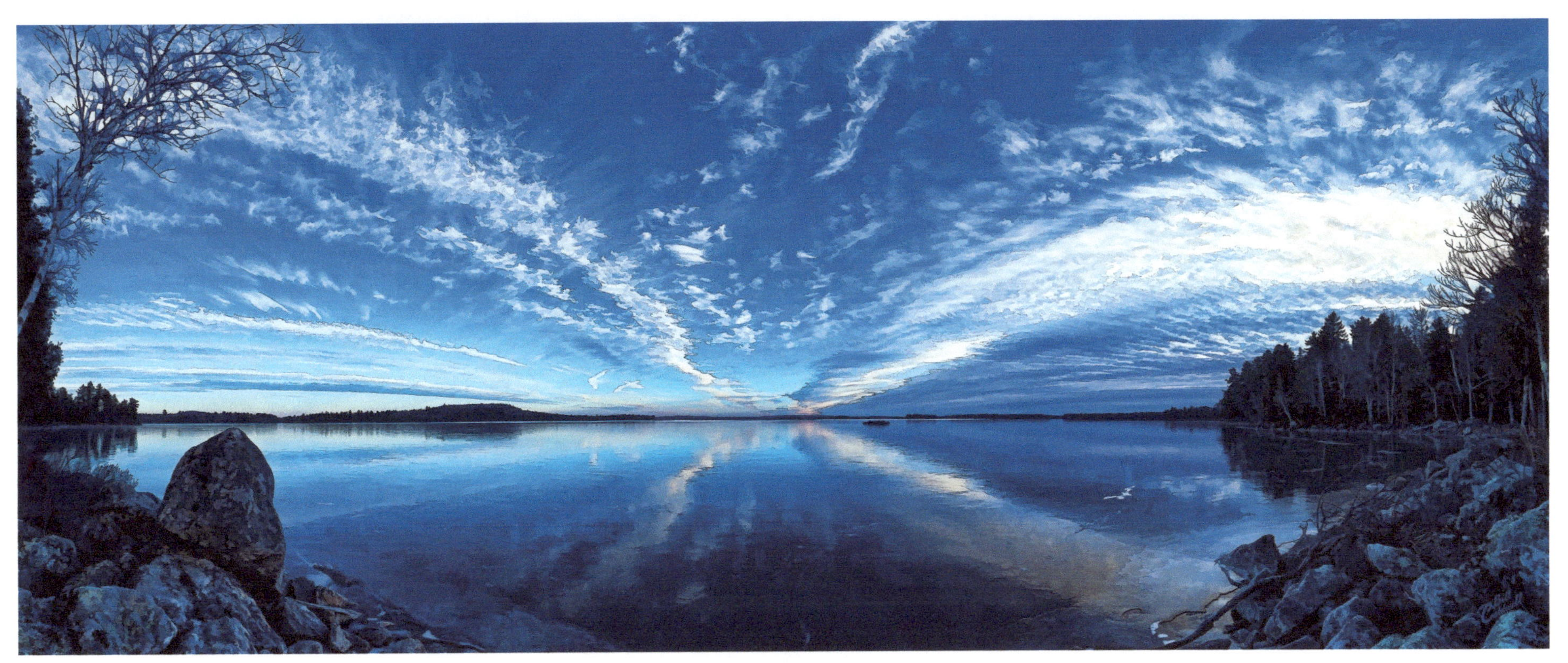

Responsible Choice

What if we all acted out of reverence for all life, the environment, and the planet as a whole?

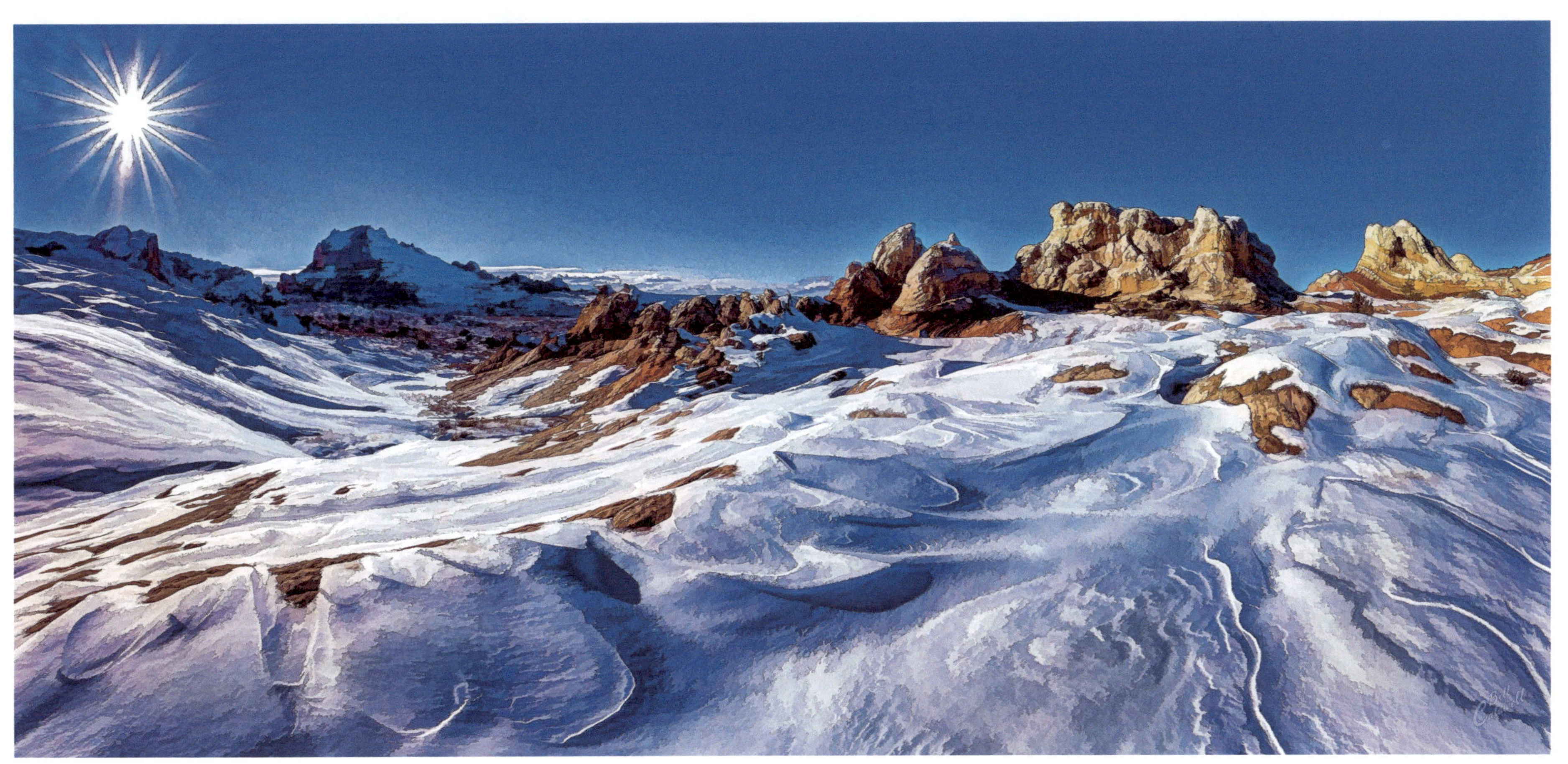

Reverence for All Life

I wonder what that world would look like?

It's not too late to change our path…

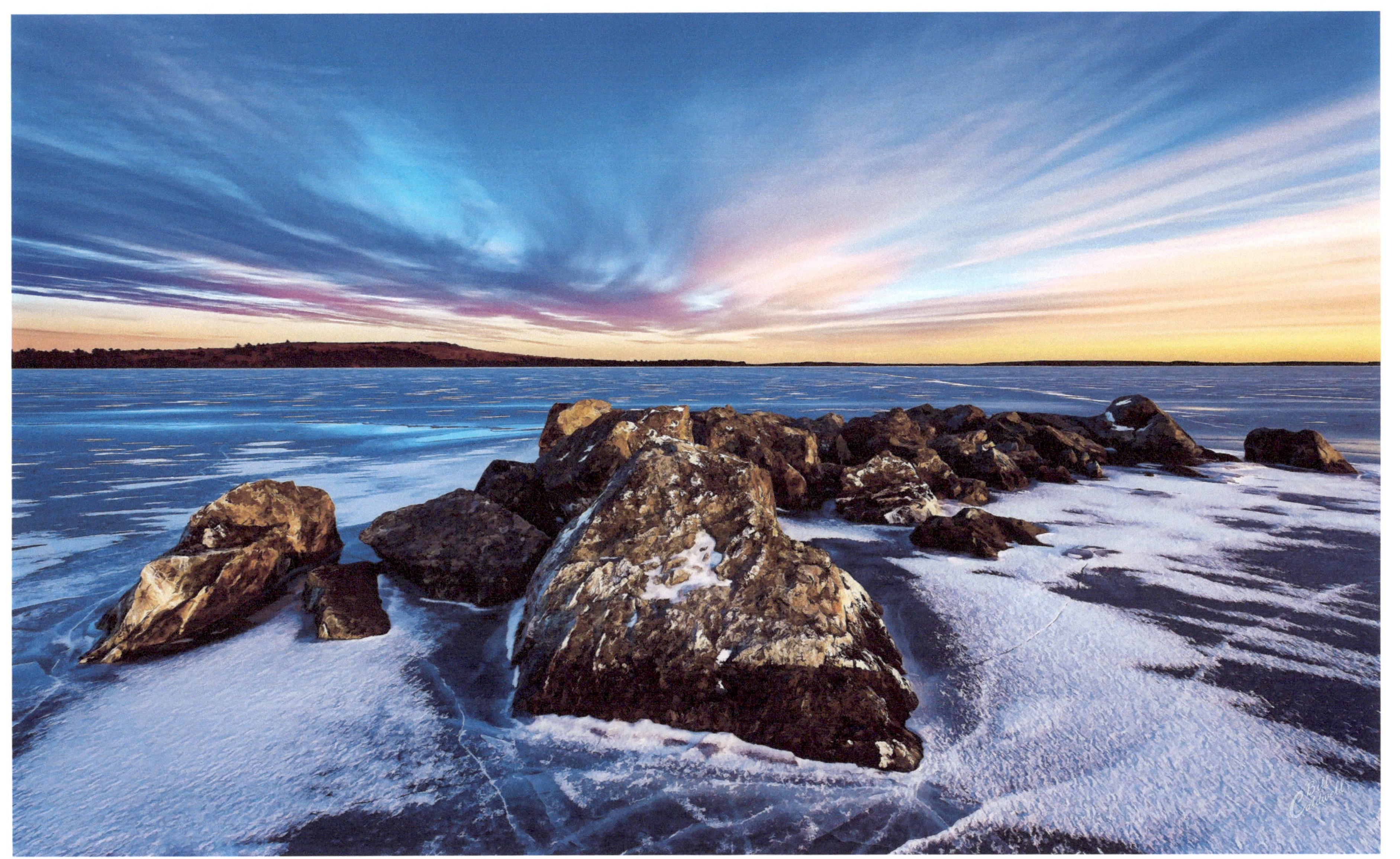

It's Not Too Late…

A Few of my Favorite Books:

Alexander, Dr. Eben, and Karen Newell. *Living in a Mindful Universe: a Neurosurgeon's Journey into the Heart of Consciousness*. Rodale, 2017.

Alexander, Dr. Eben. *Proof of Heaven: a Neurosurgeon's Journey into the Afterlife*. Simon & Schuster, 2012.

Castaneda, Carlos. *The Active Side of Infinity*. HarperCollins, 2000.

Hawkings, Steven. *A Brief History of Time*. Bantam Books, 1988.

Hicks, Esther and Jerry (and Abraham). *The Amazing Power of Deliberate Intent: Living the Art of Allowing*. Hay House, 2006.

Lomakayu, Clay. *One Noble Truth*. Circle Books, 2016.

Ruiz, Miguel. *The Four Agreements: Toltec Wisdom Collection*. Amber-Allen Pub., 1997.

Sagan, Carl. *Cosmos*. Random House, 1980.

Tolle, Eckhart. *A New Earth: Awakening to Your Life's Purpose*. Penguin Books, 2006.

Walsch, Neale Donald. *Conversations with God: an Uncommon Dialogue Book 1,2, & 3*. TarcherPerigee, 1996.

Walsch, Neale Donald. *Home with God in a Life That Never Ends: a Wondrous Message of Love in a Final Conversation with God*. Simon & Schuster, 2006.

Weiss, Brian L. *Messages from the Masters: Tapping into the Power of Love*. Grand Central Publishing, 2001.

Weiss, Brian L. *Same Soul, Many Bodies: Discover the Healing Power of Future Lives through Progression Therapy*. Free Press, 2005.

Weiss, Brian. *Many Lives, Many Masters: the True Story of a Prominent Psychiatrist, His Young Patient, and the Past-Life Therapy That Changed Both Their Lives*. Touchstone, 1988.

Zukav, Gary, and Linda Francis. *The Heart of the Soul: Emotional Awareness*. Free Press, 2001.

Zukav, Gary, et al. *The Seat of the Soul*. Simon and Schuster, 1989.

About the Author

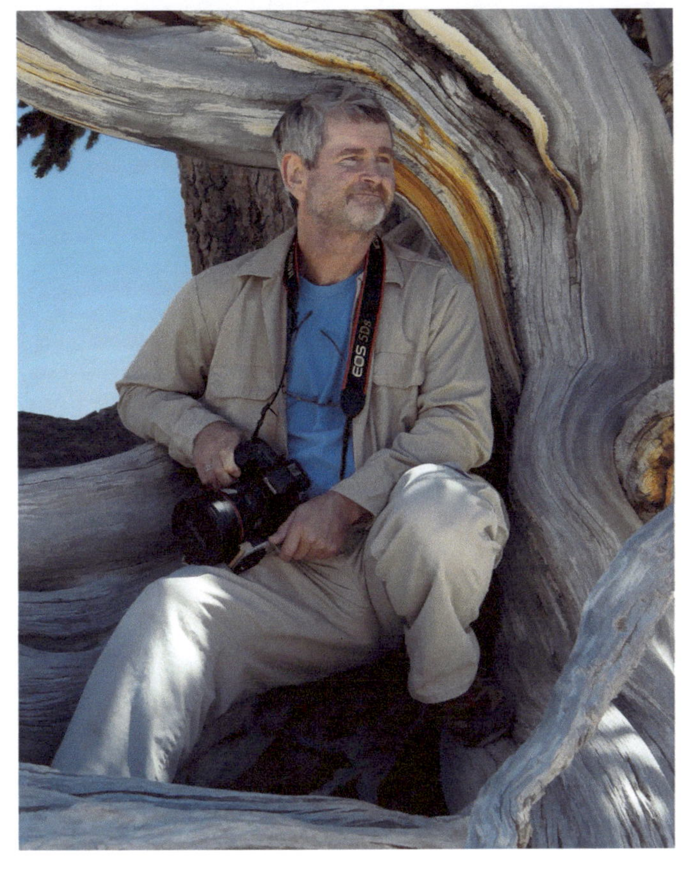

Bill Caldwell has always loved hiking and the outdoors so his artistic photography is based in the natural world—landscapes, seascapes, and macro/close-ups of flowers, leaves, rocks, and driftwood, as well as abstracts created from his macro images. After earning his BA degree in industrial and scientific photography in 1978, he spent 20 years in the US Air Force as a Combat Search and Rescue (CSAR) navigator. Now he's pursuing his lifelong love of landscape and artistic photography along with his enduring interest in spirituality. Although he's a bit of a nomad, he currently lives with his wife and cat in the Southwest and he's amazed at the stunning beauty of the Red Rock Country area as well as the surrounding region. One of the definitions of the word sacred is "worthy of or regarded with reverence, awe, or respect." In this sense, he considers these beautiful natural areas as sacred ground. He feels a strong spiritual connection to the land so his photographic art comes from a place of profound reverence and appreciation for this beautiful planet Earth. His primary intention is always to create beautifully uplifting pictures that capture the spirit of each location, and to communicate his feeling of awe and wonder when he explores and photographs the incredible spacious beauty of the natural world. You can see more of his photographic art and find more information about the pictures in this book at: www.ABeautifulSky.com.

What If

*What if all people from all lands worked
together in cooperation and collaboration?*

*What if we all set aside our political and religious
differences and worked together for the benefit of all?*

*What if we all set aside our self-interest and
hubris and made responsible choices?*

*What if we all acted out of reverence for all life,
the environment, and the planet as a whole?*

*I wonder what that world would look like?
It's not too late to change our path…*